HAL LEONARD KEYBOARD STYLE SERIES

BEBOP
JAZZ PIANO

THE COMPLETE GUIDE WITH CD!

D1546767

BY JOHN VALERIO

ISBN 0-634-03353-0

HAL•LEONARD®
CORPORATION
7777 W. BLUEMOUND RD. P.O. BOX 13819 MILWAUKEE, WI 53213

Visit Hal Leonard Online at www.halleonard.com

INTRODUCTION

What Is Bebop Jazz?

Bebop jazz is a style of music that first evolved during the 1940s. It marked the beginning of modern jazz and was revolutionary in many ways. Melodically, harmonically, and rhythmically, the music was significantly more complex than earlier forms of jazz, rewriting the rules on just about everything from how to voice a chord to how to compose a melody to how to accent a phrase.

While bebop represents the beginning of modern jazz, it is not modern jazz per se. Modal jazz, free jazz, fusion, etc. have evolved since bebop and influence contemporary jazz to one degree or another. As a style, pure bebop lasted until the mid 1950s, when it was eventually superceded by its offshoots, cool jazz and hard bop. These in turn lasted until the early 1960s when modal jazz and free jazz became dominant.

This book, then, deals with what might be termed "classic bebop"—the specific style of jazz developed by artists such as Charlie Parker, Dizzy Gillespie, Thelonious Monk, Bud Powell, Kenny Clarke, and others— which thrived from the early 1940s through the mid 1950s. While new styles come into jazz, older styles remain. Today, bebop remains the bedrock of contemporary jazz and a viable form of expression that dominates jazz curricula throughout the world.

How to Use This Book

Bebop is a complex music that can seem bewildering at first. This book offers ways of knowing and understanding what one is listening to. It provides a context and syntax for assimilation of the style.

In order to learn how to truly play bebop—or any other style, for that matter—one must listen to it. Listen to the original masters, as well as newer ones. After one becomes familiar with the music in one's ear, one can begin the study of bebop.

Each chapter in this book focuses on a particular aspect of bebop piano playing—e.g., chord voicings, chord progressions, reharmonization, comping, melodic ideas, scales, etc. Each aspect is thoroughly explored, with full examples culled from actual bebop tunes. Practice suggestions are also provided at the end of most chapters. By playing through the examples and practicing the suggested exercises, the reader should gain proficiency and fluency not only in bebop, but also in jazz playing in general.

About the CD

The accompanying CD features many of the examples in the book performed either solo or with a full band, enabling the reader to acquire a listening vocabulary as well as a reading one. Also included are combo performances of five of the tunes featured at the end of the book. These tracks can be used to practice comping and soloing in the bebop style. (To play along with the tracks without the piano part, turn down the right stereo channel.)

John Alexander: alto and tenor sax
John Valerio: piano
Lee Burrows: bass
James Baker: drums

CONTENTS

Chapter 1
HISTORY AND EVOLUTION

In order to understand and appreciate just how revolutionary bebop was as a musical style, it helps to know what came before it, as well as how the style evolved from its predecessors. Before we delve deeply into the "how to" of playing bebop jazz piano, let's take a quick look at its evolution and ancestry.

Ragtime

Jazz's immediate forerunners in the early part of the twentieth century were ragtime and blues. Ragtime was a virtuoso, written solo piano music developed by African-Americans during the 1890s. It blended traditions of Western-European music with elements of West African music into a unique original style; the harmony and form were from Europe, but the rhythmic conception was from West Africa.

Without going into detail, it's important to note that ragtime was conceived on two simultaneous layers of rhythmic activity. The left hand, for the most part, kept a steady four-beats-per-measure by alternating a bass note and chord. The right hand played melodies that were based on a pulse of eight beats per measure, which was twice the speed of the left hand. The right-hand melodies were grouped into patterns based on the African concept of additive rhythms: Rhythmic groupings and accent patterns such as 3+3+2 or 3+3+3 were played by the right while a steady four beats per measure were played by the left hand at half the speed. This led to many accented notes played by the right hand that did not coincide with the beats played by the left. (Ragtime was typically written in 2/4 time as shown. Modern practice would notate it in 2/2 time by doubling all the note values.)

The effect to Western ears was one of syncopation, but the real rhythmic concept should be understood as separate simultaneous layers. This had important ramifications for jazz, which evolved into a rhythmically multi-layered music.

Although ragtime is not jazz per se, it directly inspired it, and served as a model for jazz piano for the first forty years until bebop was born in the early 1940s. The alternating bass note-chord, steady quarter-note pulse was kept in the left hand. The right played written or improvised melodies that floated on top of the left-hand pulse.

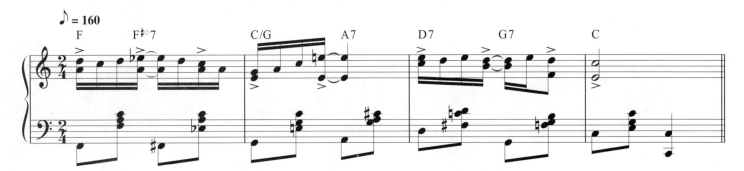

When playing accompaniment as part of a rhythm section, the pianist essentially played with two hands what he or she played with the left hand while soloing. Fills were often added, and occasionally the oom-pah, oom-pah accompaniment part was broken up with several bass note or chords in a row. It was imperative for the pianist to keep the pulse no matter what.

Blues

Blues, the other immediate forerunner of jazz, evolved on American plantations in the South during the second half of the nineteenth century. In its original form, blues was a vocal music sung by a male who accompanied himself on a guitar. The vocal practice descended from West Africa while the harmony came from Western-European music. Early blues was essentially improvised and made up on the spot.

Blues differed from ragtime in that it was improvised and had a looser rhythmic feeling to it. The accompanying guitar usually played chords derived from a major scale in a quarter-note rhythm (in 4/4 time), while the singer sang freely floating melodies on top. It's difficult to rhythmically notate an authentic blues exactly. The melodic material of early blues was derived from the so-called "blues scale." The layering effect seen in ragtime is also evident in early blues through the separate rhythmic and tonal conception of the melody and accompaniment. Blues is important in the evolution of jazz and has remained a key element for its essence. (For more on blues, see Chapter 8.)

New Orleans Jazz

Jazz itself originated in New Orleans around 1900. It evolved when musicians began "ragging the tune," which was a term used when they took a written or known tune and changed the rhythms and inflections in order to sound more like ragtime or blues. (To put it another way, ragtime piano turned into jazz piano when players infused blues and improvisation into it.) Today, we might use the term "jazzing it up." Improvisation was a key ingredient, and jazz began to "swing" through the subtle dichotomy between the syncopated melodic rhythms and the harmonic/cadential rhythms and pulse.

Ragtime seems stiff when compared to jazz. **Jelly Roll Morton** is the most important early jazz pianist; he loosened the "even subdivisions" effect of ragtime, turning "straight" eighth notes into "swing" eighth notes by playing them unevenly in a long-short manner. What formerly would be written and played as two even eighth notes would now be played as a quarter note and eighth note as part of an eighth-note triplet (♫ = ♩♪). This more relaxed attitude has stayed with jazz ever since.

Stride

Another jazz piano style known as "stride piano" grew out of ragtime and flourished in New York during the 1920s and early 1930s. This style is sometimes referred to as "Eastern ragtime" or the "Harlem piano school". The tempos could be extremely fast, and the great stride pianists had amazing left hands that were able to play the steady quarter notes at great speeds. Cross-rhythm effects were often played in the left hand by changing accents and bass-note/chord patterns. Tenths were often played instead of single notes or octaves, and, as in the New Orleans style, walking bass lines often broke up the oom-pah patterns. The right hand played chordal, octave, and single-note melodies. Unlike classic ragtime—but like New Orleans piano—stride swung, and the stride pianists improvised. **James P. Johnson** and his student **Fats Waller** were the leading stride pianists.

Swing

Swing piano style emerged during the mid 1930s with the swing big bands. While still rooted in stride style, swing piano style had a lighter touch and a looser feel. The driving accents of stride were ironed out into the even 4/4 pulse of swing. The left hand often added a tenth above the bass note—which softened the sound—and often played several bass notes in a row as "walking" tenths. The right hand became suppler, and lightning-fast runs were interspersed among single-note and chordal melodies.

Earl Hines was instrumental in transforming New Orleans and stride styles into swing style and advanced the art of jazz piano improvisation as much as Louis Armstrong did for trumpet players. Hines played horn-like lines in single notes and octaves, known as "trumpet piano," and pointed the way not only for swing but bebop pianists as well. **Teddy Wilson** and **Art Tatum** were the premiere swing pianists.

The Birth of Bebop

A radical change in jazz piano began during the early 1940s with the birth of bebop. Pianists now no longer kept a steady pulse along with the rest of the rhythm section; instead, they "comped." *Comping* refers to the playing of random-like chordal punctuations. The accompaniment rhythms were no longer steady and no longer predictable. Gone entirely was the playing of a bass part. Comping was performed with two hands when accompanying and with the left hand when soloing. **Count Basie** as well as **Earl Hines** and **Duke Ellington** were the most influential in transforming the stride-like swing style accompaniment into the comping approach. Basie was the first to consistently do so during the Swing era and served as the immediate inspiration to the bebop pianists. **Nat Cole** also was instrumental in developing a freer, lighter left-hand approach. The new style emphasized the beat less and added a new layer of rhythm to the rhythm section.

Bebop drummers also emphasized the beat less and punctuated the music by randomly playing on various drums in non-predictable ways. Bebop foreground melodies and rhythms became so complex that this less restrictive approach to rhythm-section playing became desirable and necessary. **Charlie Parker**, **Dizzy Gillespie,** and other horn players developed a highly complex melodic-rhythmic approach that featured random-like accents in their melodic lines. These accents, along with those of the pianists and drummers, added a much more complex rhythmic layering than was present in earlier styles of jazz.

Bebop pianists began imitating the harmonically complex, convoluted lines of the horn players, and single-note scalar melodies replaced the mostly arpeggiated and chordal melodies of earlier styles. Bebop players developed a complex harmonic system that relied on extended and altered chords, along with intricate chord progressions.

All of these changes were radical departures from the previous swing style, and many older players never liked or never adapted to the newer style. As with most revolutions in music history, rhythm was the key. Every aspect of rhythm, from phrasing, phrase lengths, and melodic accents to "letting go of the pulse" and rhythm-section comping, was new.

Thelonious Monk was one of the founding fathers of bebop. He, along with Dizzy Gillespie and others, developed a new harmonic system inspired by Art Tatum's innovations. He also developed a new way of voicing chords. **Bud Powell** learned Monk's voicings and later incorporated Charlie Parker's melodic approach into his piano playing and became the consummate, most imitated bebop pianist. (Although he was one of the inventors of bebop, Monk developed a unique highly original style that remained outside the "normal" way of playing.)

In the early twenty-first century, jazz, like other art forms, is looking back at its history for inspiration. Many outstanding young musicians are playing bebop in almost its pure form; almost all contemporary jazz players include at least some bebop in their repertoire. The following chapters will offer insights into the historical bebop piano style as practiced by the original bebop masters.

Chapter 2
THE BEBOP LANGUAGE

Bebop differs from earlier jazz styles in its melodic, harmonic, and rhythmic language. Like most revolutions in musical style, the most radical change was in the area of rhythm. Many swing players adapted to and adopted the harmonic language of bebop, but virtually none incorporated its rhythmic essence. This is understandable, as harmony is the most intellectual element of music and can be comprehended through study, while rhythm is a more basic intuitive element and defies formulaic scrutiny. Melody, of course, is the most prominent element of music and relies on both harmony and rhythm for its existence.

Harmony

Seventh and Sixth Chords

In traditional music, the fundamental unit of harmony is the triad; in jazz, it's the *seventh chord*—or, alternatively, the sixth. (Sixth chords are often used in place of seventh chords in jazz.) The fundamental seventh and sixth chords with the root C are shown below.

Seventh and sixth chords can be inverted to create four possible positions, or *inversions*, for each chord. A few examples follow. (These are in *closed position,* meaning the chord tones are spaced as closely as possible.)

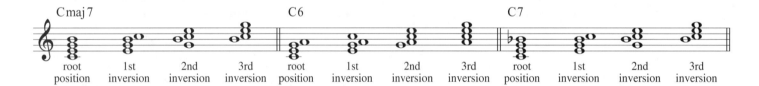

The relationship among chords is the most important aspect of harmony. Basic chord relationships are derived from their root positions on a diatonic scale, with chord qualities being determined by the superimposition of thirds derived from that scale. Roman numerals (I, II, III, etc.) are used to denote scale position. Diatonic seventh chords for the key of C major are shown below.

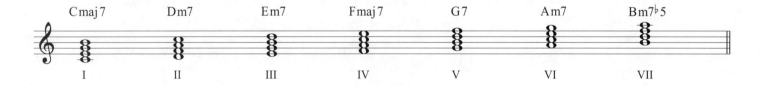

Notice that I and IV chords are major sevenths; II, III, and VI chords are minor sevenths; the V chord is a dominant seventh; and the VII chord is minor seventh flat-five chord (half-diminished seventh). This is consistent for every major key.

Diatonic seventh chords for minor keys are a bit more problematic since there are several minor scales. The most commonly used diatonic seventh chords for C minor are shown below.

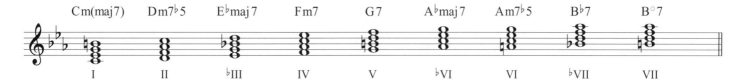

Extensions

One of the revolutions in bebop harmony was the consistent use of chord tones higher than a seventh. Ninths, elevenths, and thirteenths are regularly added by the comping pianist or are implied in bebop melodies. These *upper extensions* are obtained by adding thirds on top of the basic seventh chord. An example from a C7 follows.

As with triads and seventh chords, one can construct diatonic ninth chords from a major scale. An example in C major is shown below.

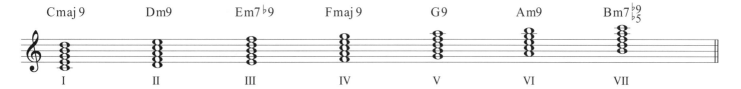

Diatonic eleventh and thirteenth chords in C major follow.

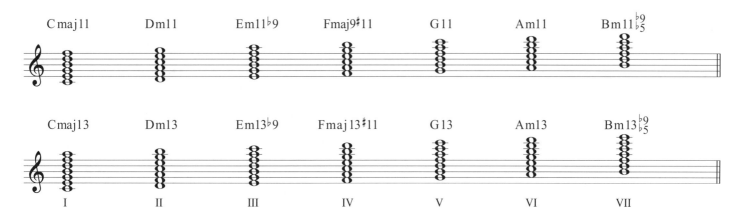

Notice the complex sounds that result from playing these chords. These chords are rarely heard in these positions as simultaneously sounding chords but are often voiced in other ways and/or implied in bebop melodic lines.

Charlie Parker is often quoted when emphasizing the importance of extended chord tones in bebop. He refers to one night when practicing "Cherokee," he discovered that by playing the higher intervals of chords in creating melodies, he came alive. In other words, he stumbled upon the essence of the new music that was to become bebop. (Of course, it was also his unique rhythmic approach that gave birth to bebop.)

Alterations

The seventh chord remains the fundamental harmonic unit in bebop, but additional chord tones (upper partials) are freely added in melodies. In addition, bebop melodies often rely on *altered* chord tones. Thus, the upper chord extensions (also known as *tensions*) are often raised or lowered by a half step. The possibilities for harmonic coloration become almost limitless when these options are employed. Below are samples of some of the more commonly used extended and altered extended chords for each basic seventh and sixth chord quality.

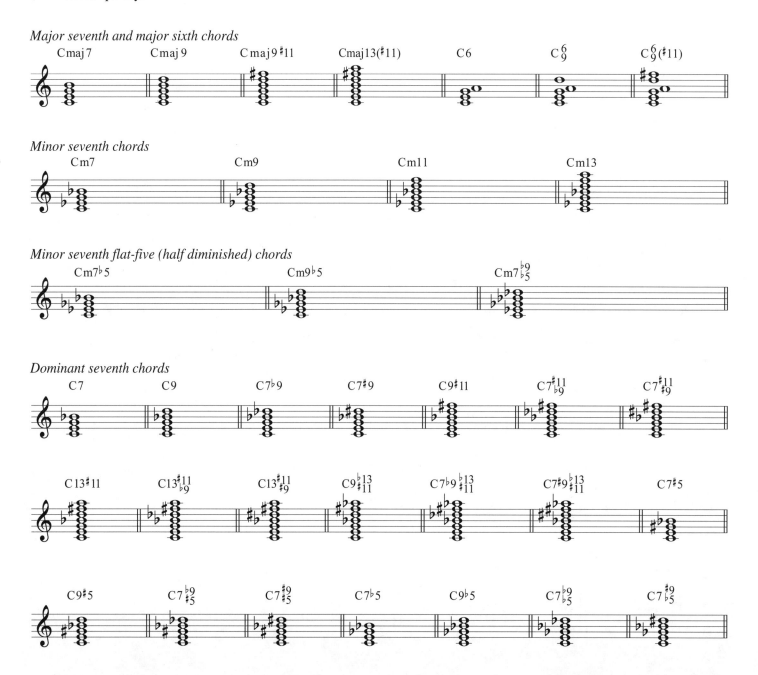

Various elevenths and thirteenths may also be added to C7#5 and C7♭5 chords given above. The flatted fifth is considered to be a crucial characteristic of bebop harmonic practice. One may think of the flat five as a sharp eleven in most cases.

Interlocking Triads & Seventh Chords

Thinking of the upper extensions of chords can be simplified by breaking the chords into two separate parts: lower and upper. These separate units can be thought of as superposed or interlocking triads and seventh chords. For example, a C major ninth chord can be constructed by placing a G major triad on top of a C major seventh chord, or by placing an E minor seventh chord on top of a C major seventh chord. The following example shows how this can be done with some common ninth, eleventh, and thirteenth chords.

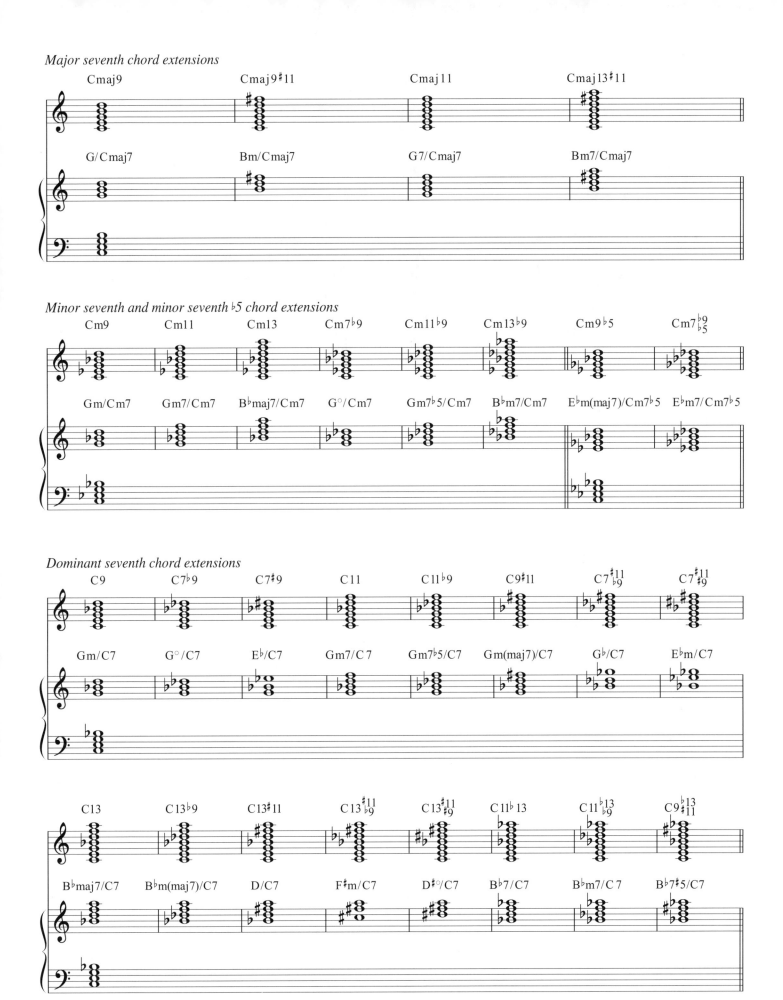

Harmonic-Melodic Improvisation

Keep in mind that these extensions and alterations most often occur in melodic lines and not as chord voicings. Melodic lines often consist of arpeggiated upper chord partials. A sample melodic line follows.

Notice that the notes over the Dm7 chord arpeggiate chord tones 3–5–7–9, and, after a chromatic descending motion beginning on ♭13 over the G7, the notes over the Em7 chord outline chord tones 5–7–9–11 and lead to ♭9-7 over the A7. This is a typical bebop line that relies on extended and altered tones. One can think of the notes on the Dm7 as a superimposed Fmaj7 chord and the notes over the Em7 as a superimposed Bm7 chord. Regardless of how one thinks of these formations, the effects are the same.

The next example is based on similar principles. The extended and altered chords implied by the melody can be represented as C9–F13#11–B♭9#11–Cmaj7.

The upper structures of the chords implied by this melodic line can be related to the basic harmony as follows. Again, it is not important how one thinks of these structures but only that one is aware of how these complex harmonic formations work within the context of the melodic lines.

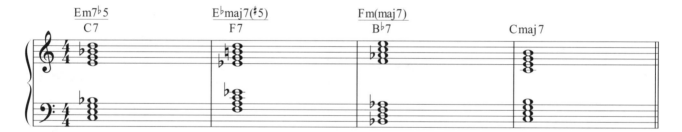

Rhythm

Rhythm is a key element in the bebop style. It works on many levels and occurs on many simultaneous layers.

Note Duration

The most obvious rhythmic layer occurs on the melodic surface—that is, the note durations of the melody itself. In medium- to fast-tempo tunes, eighth notes predominate while eighth-note triplets and sixteenth notes are used to a lesser extent. This is not to say that quarter notes and half notes, etc. are not also used. The eighth note, however, is the basic melodic rhythmic unit. The following example shows a typical bebop melody with typical melodic rhythms.

TRACK 1

NOTE: Bebop is generally played with what might be called a "light swing feel." The eighth notes are often swung—that is, played unevenly—but less so than tunes from the Swing era. The closest approximation to this feel is best described as ♪=♪. In practice, the amount of unevenness depends on the player and the tempo of a performance. Faster tempos tend to yield straighter eighth notes.

Phrasing

Notice how the previous phrase begins and ends on an eighth note in between beats. This is very typical of bebop phrases. Phrases can begin and end on any beat or between any beat. This and the variety of melodic rhythms are two of the key differences between bebop and swing styles. Swing melodies tend to be rhythmically more consistent than bebop melodies and tend to begin and end exactly on beats more often. The following example is a straightened-out swing version of the previous phrase. Notice the different impact that it has.

TRACK 2

Accents

Accents are an important aspect of rhythm. While swing melodies tend to have regular accentuation patterns, placing emphasis on the strong beats for the most part, bebop melodies are characterized by uneven and unpredictable accents within the melodic line. The swing version of the previous phrase might be accented as follows.

TRACK 3

Next is an example of how the bebop version of the phrase might by accented.

TRACK 4

Contour

Although the accents for the melodic line in the previous example are not even, the contour of the melody is rather predictable in that it has peaks on the third beat of every measure. This makes the phrase still somewhat related to swing style, which tends to put accents and peaks on beats 1 and 3. The phrase can be turned into a more idiosyncratic bebop line by shifting everything one beat forward. The phrase would then start on the "and" of 2 instead of the "and" of 1.

TRACK 5

Notice how the rhythm is more complex because the line peaks on beat 4 of each measure instead of beat 3.

Phrase Lengths

A crucial aspect of bebop rhythmic practice is the use of varied phrase lengths. Whereas more traditional forms of jazz tend to group phrases into units of two, four, and eight measures—following the cadences of the underlying chord progression—bebop phrases tend to be uneven and varied in length. A typical bebop melody may contain phrase lengths of one-and-a-half, two-and-a-half, three, five, and half measures, etc. This adds to the rhythmic complexity of bebop. A typical eight-bar bebop progression follows.

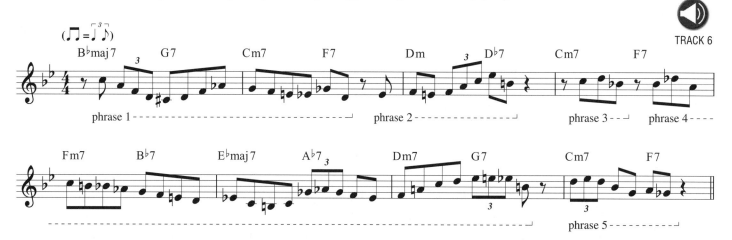

Notice how the shorter phrases tend to create tension while the longer ones tend to release tension. Charlie Parker was a master at using this principle effectively. Notice also that the phrases in the above example end with descending two-note figures. This is very characteristic of bebop; in fact, the word "bebop" is thought to have derived from the sound of these abrupt two-note phrase endings.

Melody

Melody in bebop relies on the genre's harmonic and rhythmic practice and does not exist as a separate element. Bebop melodies most often imply harmonic function, but as we have seen, the harmonic implications are not always those of the given material. Because of this quasi-harmonic improvisation that goes along with the melodic improvisation, bebop melodies are difficult to analyze in traditional terms. In traditional melodic-harmonic analysis, each melody note is heard in relation to the prevailing chord and is therefore classified into one of two categories: harmonic tone or non-harmonic tone. Non-harmonic tones are further classified as passing tones, neighboring tones, suspensions, etc. The problem with analyzing bebop melodies in this manner is determining which tones are harmonic or non-harmonic. If we allow all extensions and alterations as possible chord tones, what are left as non-chord tones?

Also, if we allow for spontaneous chord superimposition upon existing chords, do we analyze the melody in relation to the implied chords or the given chords? A good answer might be: It depends on the context and each individual circumstance. But who determines these—the player, the analyst, or the listener? All three may come up with different but equally valid perceptions. For our purposes here, we should probably go with the player since this is an approach for playing bebop.

Traditional analysis often is an ineffective tool when it comes to jazz. That's because jazz is not constructed like traditional music. Jazz is a layered music; it consists of simultaneous layers of quasi-independent activity. Each layer proceeds on its own, at the same time as the other layers, but not necessarily tied to the other layers. What holds all of the layers together is the tune itself. Everyone is playing the same tune at the same time, but each one may be thinking of the music in different contexts.

Several of the following chapters will focus on bebop common melodic practice. One must keep in mind that, in bebop, melody is a manifestation of harmony, but the harmonic implications of a melody do not always coincide with the prevailing harmony. These points should become clearer as one reads through the following chapters.

Chapter 3
CHORDS AND VOICINGS

Bebop chords and chord voicings are more complex than those used in earlier jazz—but relatively simple compared to later styles of jazz. In early jazz, pianists played chords in root position most of the time and employed a limited number of voicings. The bebop pianist, however, discovered new ways of voicing chords and, because of the relative simplicity of these voicings, freed up the melodic-rhythmic impulse of the music.

Bebop piano styles are usually associated with playing in a group situation. The pianist either accompanies other players or is featured as a soloist within the group. Solo or unaccompanied bebop piano was relatively rare, and when pianists played unaccompanied, they usually played the same as when a rhythm section was present.

The bebop pianist generally uses two-handed voicings when accompanying and left-hand voicings when soloing. Open voicings are generally employed whether playing chords with one or two hands. (An *open voicing* consists of an arrangement of notes that contain at least one gap between two adjacent chord tones.)

Four-Note Voicings

Two-handed voicings are easiest described by the left-hand structure. This is also convenient because voicings for the left hand alone are essentially the same as the left-hand structure of voicings for two hands.

Root and Seventh

The most common left-hand structure used in bebop, from the lowest to highest notes, is root and seventh—or root and sixth if a sixth chord is used. This leaves the right hand to fill in the remaining notes. When a simple four-note seventh or sixth chord is desired, these notes would be the third and fifth. These voicings will be referred to as *1–7–3–5* or *1–6–3–5* voicings. Examples for the basic chord qualities on the root C follow.

Root and Fifth

Other common voicings are derived from the left-hand structure of root and fifth. While the left always plays the root and fifth in that order from the bottom, the right-hand structure can be either third-and-seventh or seventh-and-third. These voicings will be referred to as *1–5–3–7* and *1–5–7–3* voicings. Examples of both forms for the root C follow.

Root and Third (or Tenth)

When a root-and-third structure is used in the left-hand, the right hand usually leaves out the fifth and plays the seventh and the ninth. Since the fifth is not present, this voicing is not always practical for chord qualities that rely on a flatted or sharped fifth. These voicings will be referred to as *1–3–7–9* voicings.

The root-third structure in the left hand can be extended to the interval of a tenth without changing the fundamental structure of the voicing. The sonority, however, is quite different.

Generally speaking, ninths function unobtrusively. One should be careful, however, when choosing a natural, flat, or sharp ninth for dominant chords. Melody and tonality are key factors in this regard. For instance, in a minor key, when progressing from a dominant V to a minor I, a flat ninth is usually more appropriate. If a blues scale effect is desired, a sharp ninth will work well on the dominant.

II-V-I PROGRESSIONS

Chords do not work in isolation but rather in logical progressions. The relationship among chords is as important as the chords themselves. Chord voicings often work together in systematic ways. For instance, *1–7–3–5* voicings often alternate with *1–3–7–9* voicings when chord roots move down by fifths. Following is an example for II–V–I progressions in C major and C minor. Both sevenths and sixths are used for I chords in these examples.

Tenths can be used in place of the root-third structure in the left hand.

The same principle can work starting with a *1–3–7–9* voicing on the first chord and a *1–7–3–5* voicing for the next, etc. The following example shows both variations for II–V–I in C major only.

The four-note voicings used above allow for fifths and ninths to be easily altered as necessary or desired. Two examples follow.

ALTERNATING II-V'S

The technique of alternating 1-7 left-hand voicings with 1-3(10) voicings can be applied to other progressions that contain chords whose roots move down by fifth. Alternating II–V progressions in keys that move down by whole steps are an example of such a progression. If this pattern continues through six keys, it will circle back on itself and start to repeat. Notice that each chord root moves down by fifth while each II-V movement moves down by whole step. The next example presents this pattern in six keys, descending in whole steps beginning with a II–V progression C major.

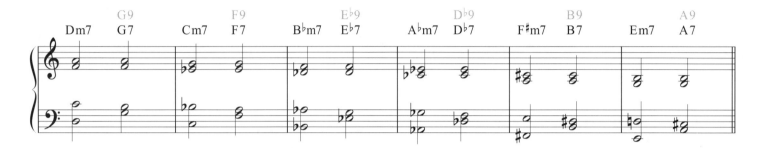

This pattern can be started in any of the remaining six major keys to complete all twelve major keys. The next example will show the remaining six keys but will use V♭9 voicings for variety.

Reversing the voicings and beginning with 1–3(10)–7–9 and alternating with 1–7–3–5 produces a similar result. Registral considerations will dictate where to start these patterns on the keyboard. The next example demonstrates this for six keys beginning with a II-V progression in G♭ major.

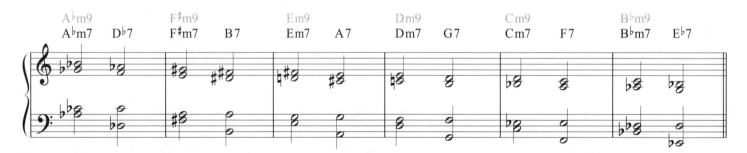

The next cycle uses 1-10 left-hand voicing (in place of 1-3) and V7♯5 chords. The remaining six keys are demonstrated.

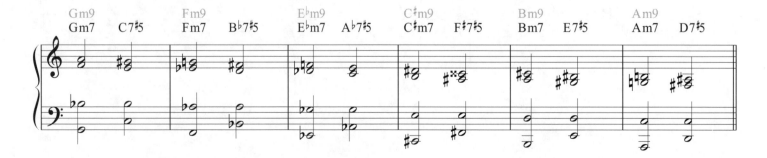

MORE VOICING COMBINATIONS

The previously mentioned 1–5–3–7 and 1–5–7–3 voicings can work systematically as well as the previous few examples. Smooth voice leading can result by alternating the right-hand 3–7 structure with the 7–3 structure when chord roots move down by fifth. Notice that the left hand always plays a fifth in this system.

As before, a II–V–I progression serves as an example.

The right-hand voicings in the examples above form what are referred to as *guide tones*. The third and the seventh of each successive chord alternate: The third of Dm7 leads to the seventh of G7, which leads to the third of Cmaj7, etc. This kind of guide-tone movement can be applied for smooth voicing in connecting chords whose roots are a fifth apart. The concept is also useful when connecting melody notes.

The same voicing formula can be applied in minor keys.

The same kind of alternating right-hand voicings work with any descending fifth motion, such as the II-V progressions in descending whole steps demonstrated previously (with 1–7–3–5 and 1–3–7–9 voicings). As an example, a series of dominant seventh chords descending down the circle of fifths follows. The right-hand voicing is reversed in the second set.

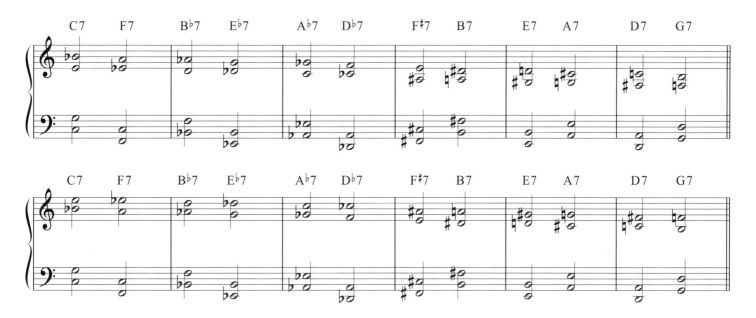

Three-Note Voicings

Three-note voicings can be used for seventh chords by dropping one note. The dropped note is usually the fifth. In practice, typical three-note voicings are derived from the four-note, 1–5–3–7 or 1–5–7–3 voicings by simply dropping the fifth. Examples of II–V–I progressions in C major and C minor follow. Notice that the guide tones are clearly exposed in the right hand.

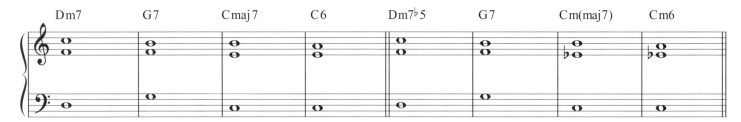

Dominant seventh three-note voicings going down the circle of fifths follow.

Five-Note Voicings

Notes can be added to the basic four-note open voicings to create richer, more complex harmonies. Ninths are usually added to major and minor sevenths, and ninths and/or elevenths and thirteenths are usually added to dominant sevenths.

Major Chords

Major seventh and sixth chords with added ninths are shown below.

Minor Chords

The same principle can be used for minor sevenths and minor seventh flat-five chords. The ninth on the m7♭5 chord used here is a major ninth; a minor ninth could also be used. One should be mindful of melody and tonality when using ninths with these chords.

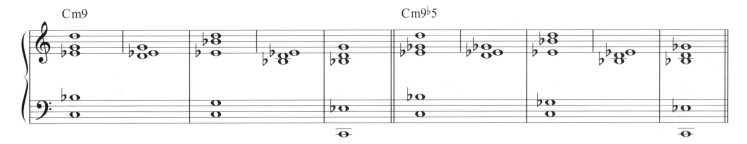

Dominant Chords

Dominant seventh chords offer the most possibilities for alterations. In the examples below, the ninth can be natural, flat, or sharp. Also, thirteenths and elevenths can be added and altered. A few sample voicings follow.

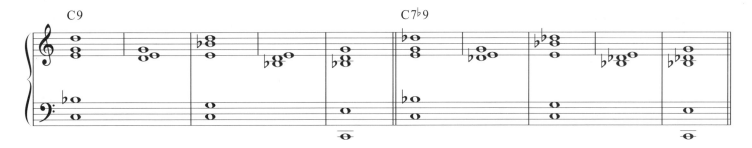

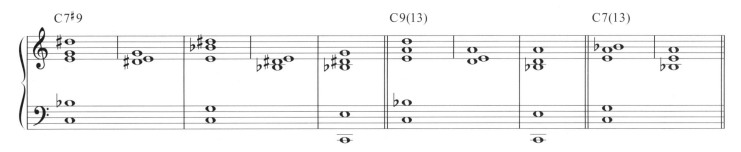

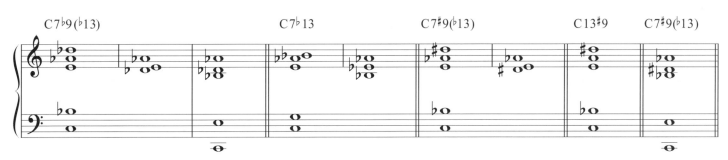

MIXED PROGRESSIONS

Smooth voice leading can be achieved with five-note voicings as easily as with four-note voicings. II–V–I progressions work well with 1–7–3–5 and 1–3–7–9 II–V–I formula when a ninth is added to the II chord and held over into the V chord, becoming a thirteenth. Here, the right-hand structure can move down a step for a smooth transition to the I chord with an added ninth.

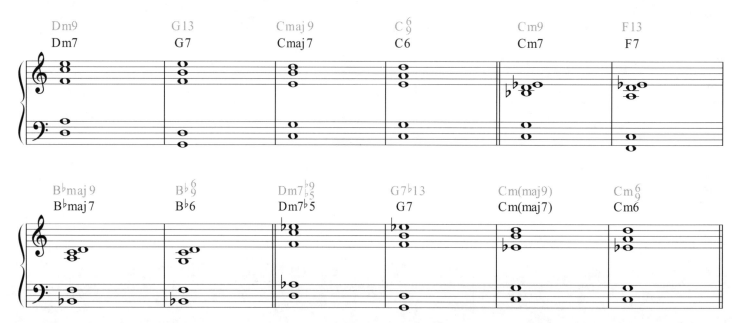

Adding the same notes to alternating root-fifth voicings achieves a similar result for the right hand.

For more ideas on adding extensions and alterations to chords, and a better idea of how these voicings can be applied, refer to the two-handed comping examples of Chapter 7.

Five-, Six- and Seven-Note Voicings

The four- and five-note voicings shown previously have no notes that are doubled. Bebop pianist often will double notes when playing chords with two hands. Overall sound quality, density of texture, and tessitura are determining factors in choosing these voicings. Below are offered a few examples of five-, six-, and seven-note voicings. Notice that most are essentially five-note voicings with doubled notes.

I chords – major sevenths and sixth voicings*

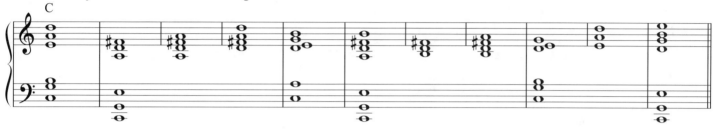

*Minor I chord voicings can be derived from the major voicings above by lowering the third to E♭.

II chords – minor sevenths and minor ♭5 voicings

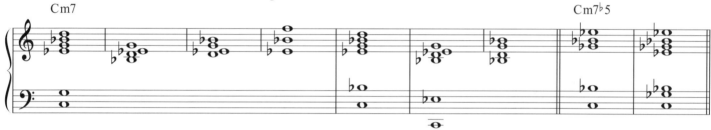

V chords – dominant seventh voicings

Left-Hand Voicings

In the pure bebop style, when the pianist solos in a group or in a solo piano performance, the left hand usually accompanies a single-note melodic line in the right hand with simple two- or three-note voicings. These voicings are usually based on the left-hand portion of the two-handed voicings discussed previously. Root-and-seventh is the most often used voicing, followed in frequency by root-and-third (or tenth). Root-and-sixth is sometimes used for major or minor I chords. Root-and-fifth is used less often. These stripped-down kinds of voicings give less specific harmonic information and were desirable because they gave more leeway for harmonic alterations.

Two-Note

The following example shows some typical two-note voicings.

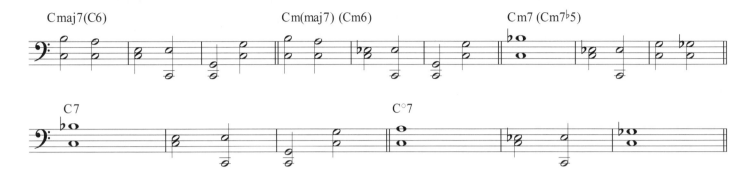

Three-Note

The next example shows some typical three-note voicings.

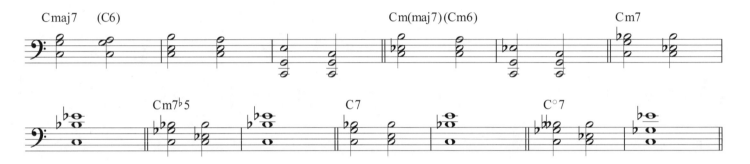

Four-Note

Sometimes, though not often, full four-note root position or inverted seventh chords are used in the left hand.

3rd and 7th

Sometimes, though not often, roots are left out, and just the third and seventh are played.

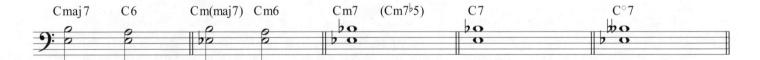

Modern jazz pianists often employ so-called "rootless voicings." This allows for more freedom for the rhythm section in general and more harmonic and coloristic possibilities. This is essentially a post-bebop development that evolved during the mid 1950s and is, by and large, not applicable to the historic original bebop conception described in this book.

The following chapters of this book will present a variety of bebop-style voicings in various contexts. See Chapter 4 for characteristic chord progressions and Chapter 7 for comping ideas.

An essential practice regimen consists of playing chords, voicings, melodic figures and patterns, etc. in an organized systematic routine. This and succeeding chapters will offer suggestions to accomplish that goal.

Practice Cycles

Any practice item such as scales, arpeggios, chords voicings, chord progressions, melodic patterns, etc. should be practiced in all twelve keys or from all twelve roots. The following cycles of keys and/or roots offer systematic ways of doing this.

Circle of Fifths

Play each scale, arpeggio, chord voicing, chord progression, melodic pattern, etc. in the order of descending fifths. For example, play the 1–7–3–5 voicing for a Cmaj7, and continue the same voicing for each root around the circle of *descending fifths*. Note that although the term descending fifth is used here, the chords may actually move up a fourth rather than down a fifth. This is because a descending fifth inverts to an ascending fourth. The choice of going up or down depends on the sound quality and clarity of the given notes.

An example of major seventh chord voicings played in the circle of descending fifths follows. (The same process can be applied to the circle of ascending fifths or descending fourths.)

An example of a chord progression played through a circle of descending fifths follows. This is a major II-V-I progression using a voicing formula found in this chapter. (The same process can be applied to the circle of ascending fifths or descending fourths.)

Whole Steps

Play each scale, arpeggio, chord voicing, chord progression, melodic pattern, etc. in the order of descending whole steps. Since a descending cycle of whole steps will create a whole tone scale and circle back on itself after six moves, two different cycles are needed to accommodate all twelve keys or roots. The following example demonstrates this for 1–7–3–5 voicings of minor seventh chords. (The same process can be applied to ascending whole steps.)

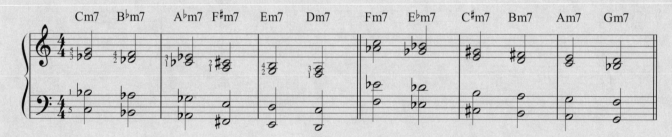

As before, chord progressions can be practiced using whole-step cycles. Below is an example for one whole-step cycle of major II–V–I progressions using a formula for the 1-5 voicings in the left hand. This process should be continued for the other whole-step cycle of keys: E♭–D♭–B–A–G–F. (The same process can be applied to ascending whole steps.)

Half Steps

Play each scale, arpeggio, chord voicing, chord progression, melodic pattern, etc. in the order of ascending half steps. The following demonstrates this with 1–5–3–7 voicings of dominant seventh chords. (The same process can be applied to descending half steps.)

The following presents major II–V progressions played in ascending half steps.

The reader should practice all of the chord voicings and chord progressions presented in this chapter by playing them through all of the cycles.

Chapter 4
HARMONY AND CHORD PROGRESSIONS

Not only were bebop chords themselves more complex than those used in earlier jazz, the chord progressions were as well. Bebop players loved to fill in static harmonic areas with harmonic movement. Tenor saxophonist Coleman Hawkins and especially pianist Art Tatum were the most influential players to develop this technique during the Swing era. Bebop musicians tend to favor a faster harmonic rhythm. Thus, extra chords are often added to pre-existing tunes and chord progressions to create not only more harmonic movement but also more challenging structures for improvisation. This process could be preplanned or improvised. Reharmonization is a characteristic feature of bebop. This chapter will present a few of the standard harmonic devices favored by bebop players.

Harmonic Embellishment

Harmonic embellishment is the process of changing one chord into two or more complementary chords. In this process, a new chord is placed before or after the given chord. The basic functions remain the same although the progression is embellished with new chords. New harmonic movement is created but within the same structural framework. This is a similar process to melodic ornamentation, where individual notes are embellished with decorative tones (see Chapter 5). Harmonic embellishment can occur in four different ways, as described below.

Displacement

V chords (dominant sevenths) are often displaced temporarily by their preceding II chords (minor sevenths). I chords (major sevenths or sixths) are often followed by their VI chords (minor sevenths). The following example shows how a I–V progression can be transformed into a I–VI–II–V through this process.

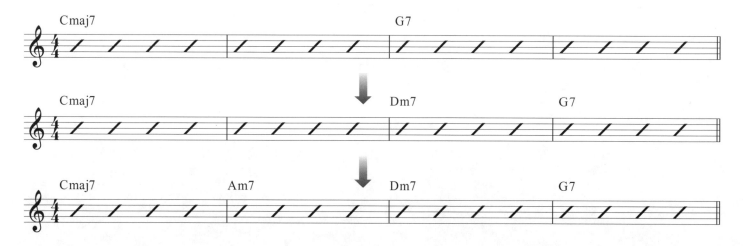

The chord progression has been changed, but essentially the harmonic motion is I–V.

Neighbor Chords

Another common type of harmonic embellishment is neighbor chord motion. Here, any chord can be embellished by slipping the chord up or down by half step and then back to its original position. An example of this process follows.

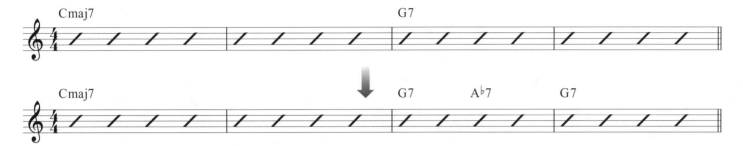

Appoggiatura Chords

Another type of harmonic embellishment is the appoggiatura chord, a chord that momentarily replaces a similar chord a half step higher or lower. (Unlike a neighbor chord, the appoggiatura precedes the chord it embellishes.) The process is demonstrated below.

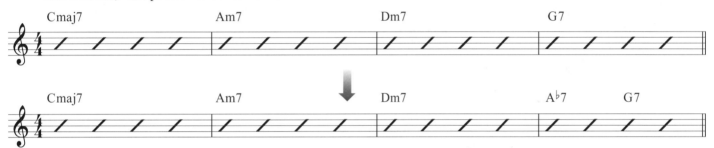

Entire chord groups can be embellished in a similar way. In the following example, the II–V chords of measures 3 and 4 are embellished by a II–V progression a half step above.

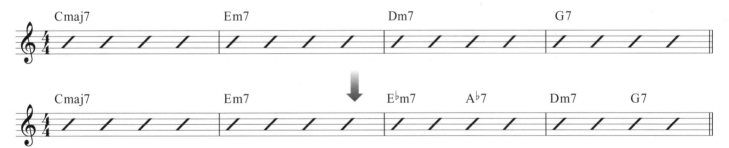

Suspended Chords

Suspended chords offer another method for harmonic embellishment. In this case, a chord is held over to where the next chord would ordinarily begin and only the root of the new chord is played. The suspended chord may or may not resolve to the implied next chord. There are two suspended chords in the follow example. The first one does not resolve, but the second one does resolve (to a G7).

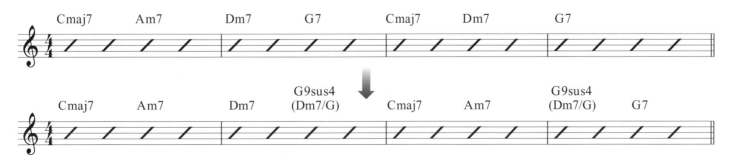

Harmonic Elaboration

Harmonic elaboration occurs when additional chords are added to basic chord progressions. This process differs from harmonic embellishment in that, here, chords are added as connecting material rather than decorative material. Often these processes overlap, and some chord additions can be thought of in either way.

Circle-of-Fifths Progressions

The key to understanding much harmonic elaboration in jazz is the *circle of fifths*. The circle (or cycle) of fifths is a graphic representation of the most fundamental harmonic relationship in tonal music: the descending fifth. The most common chord root movement is by descending fifth. The pillars upon which the whole tonal system, regardless of style and era, is built are the V-I relationship. What makes the tonal system so versatile is the extension of this principle to other chord movements, such as III-IV or I-IV, and the principle of modulation or changing keys. Modulation occurs when a new tonic is created by emphatically establishing a new V–I relationship.

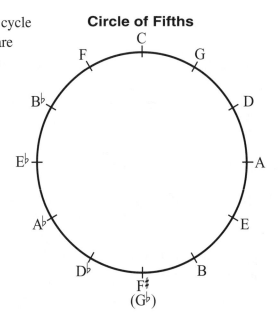

Circle of Fifths

One can arrange fifths around a circle since they naturally cycle through all twelve pitches before repeating. Descending fifths are derived by moving counterclockwise along the circle. The chord qualities may vary, as well as the length of progressions going around the circle. The most common progression used in jazz is the II–V–I progression. In the key of C major, for example, this would be Dm7–G7–Cmaj7. One can see on the circle-of-fifths chart that one can follow D to G to C by going counterclockwise. Any II–V–I progression in any key will work. For instance, one can circle counterclockwise from C to F to B♭ for a II–V–I progression in B♭ major, which is Cm7–F7–B♭maj7. Fifth relationships work regardless of the chord qualities.

CONNECTING I TO V

One can use the circle of descending fifths to elaborate otherwise static chord progressions by choosing a target chord and working backwards. The embellished I-V progression at the start of this chapter may also be seen as a circle-of-fifths harmonic elaboration. Notice the fifths by going backwards from the G7 chord (A–D–G).

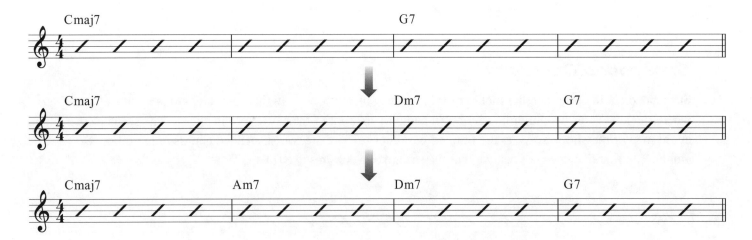

One can further elaborate on this progression by changing the qualities of the II chord and/or the VI chord to dominant seventh chords. The root movement stays the same, but the functions now change. A dominant seventh chord is usually a V chord. (There are exceptions to this in blues and some modal contexts.) Thus a D7 here would be a V of G (V of V). An A7 would be a V of D (V of II). These chords in this case do not signal a modulation, but rather a tonicization of II and V respectively. *Tonicization* puts a slight emphasis or focus on the target chords without actually changing keys. In this case, the target chords are never really reached because the dominant chords resolve into other dominant chords. In other words, the goals are thwarted, and replaced by dominant chords on the same root as the implied target chords. This is a common process in tonal music.

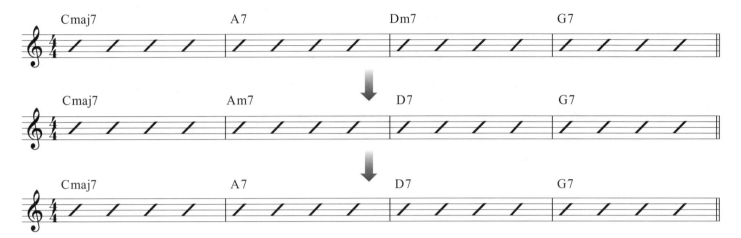

CONNECTING I TO II

This same principle can be applied to connecting a Imaj7 or I6 chord to IIm7 chord. Working backward using the circle of fifths, we can derive a II–V of II, Em7–A7, and a V of Em7, B7.

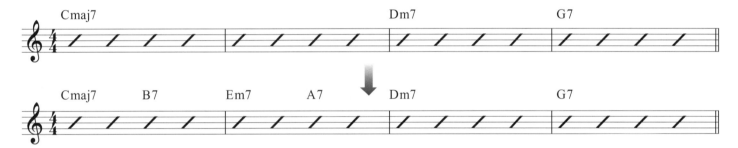

CONNECTING I TO IV

The circle of fifths can be extended when connecting a I to a IV chord over a four-measure span as follows. The fifths are arranged here as a series of II–V's. This progression is commonly used in blues tunes.

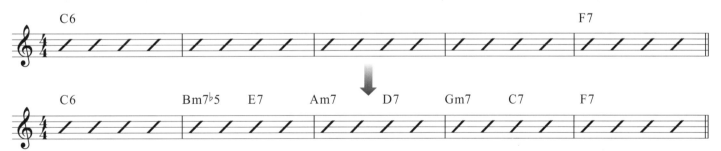

Passing Chords

Chord progressions can be elaborated through the use of passing chords. Passing chords are chords that are a whole step or half step between two other chords.

Diatonic chords are often used to connect chords that are a third apart. In the following example, a diatonic passing chord (Dm7) is used to connect I to III. This is a variation on the circle-of-fifths progression shown previously.

Chromatic chords, especially diminished sevenths, are often used to connect two chords that are a major second apart. In the following example, diminished seventh chords connect ascending diatonic seventh chords, and minor sevenths connect descending diatonic chords.

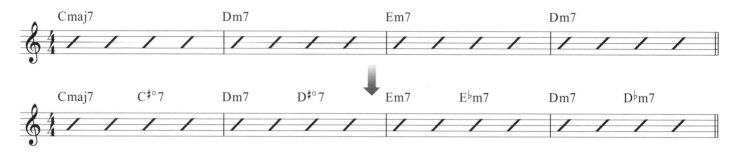

Harmonic Substitution

Harmonic substitution occurs when one chord is replaced with a different chord. This process differs from harmonic embellishment because, here, a new chord replaces an existing chord rather than preceding or following it.

The most common substitution principle used in jazz is known as *tritone substitution*. A tritone is an interval that spans three whole steps. The term is used to avoid confusion between the interval of a diminished fifth and an augmented fourth, which both span a tritone but have different enharmonic spellings. A tritone inverts to a tritone, although the interval theoretically changes from one to the other. No matter what one calls these intervals, they are all tritones.

The principle of tritone substitution is the process of replacing one chord with another chord whose root is a tritone away. This is most commonly done with dominant chords. Therefore, a D♭7 chord can substitute for a G7 chord, or a C7 can be replaced by an F♯7, etc. D♭7 and G7 are not as far apart harmonically as one might think. They share two crucial notes in common, which also happen to be a tritone apart. The third and seventh of each chord are enharmonically identical, in reverse order—B and F for G7, and F and C♭ for D♭7.

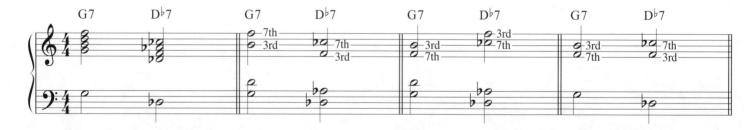

Traditionally, the third and seventh of a dominant seventh chord are the most important notes. They define the key center through their tendency to resolve to the root and third of a tonic chord. Jazz musicians exploit the ambiguity of the tritone within a dominant seventh chord by making the two chords that share the same tritone interchangeable.

The dominant seventh tritone interchangeability is further strengthened when altered notes are used. The notes in G7♭5 are enharmonically identical with those in D♭7♭5. Also, when a ♭9 is used, the top four notes of each chord are enharmonically identical. Notice that the top four notes of a dominant ♭9 form a diminished seventh chord. For tritone-related dominant ♭9 chords, these diminished seventh chords are enharmonically identical.

Notice that the only difference between the two chords above is the root. One can freely substitute for the other while everything else remains intact. One can see and hear the similarity of the two chords even though their roots are quite different.

Tritone substitution often occurs during II–V–I progressions. By using a tritone sub for the V chord, we have II–♭II–I progression. An example of the process follows. The last progression shows the similarity between V7♭9 and ♭II7.

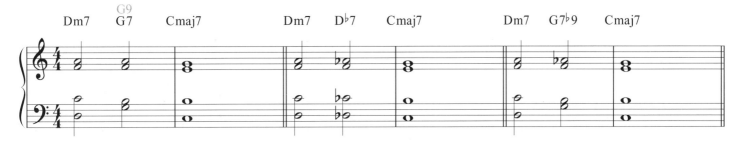

When connecting a Imaj7 or I6 chord to a IIm7 chord, the circle-of-fifths progression shown earlier can be modified by using a tritone sub for the B7. This progression is more commonly used than the previous version.

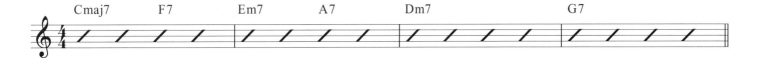

The basic I–VI–II–V progression can be modified though the use of tritone subs. Tritone subs can be used for any of the dominant chords given in the first progression given below. Several examples follow.

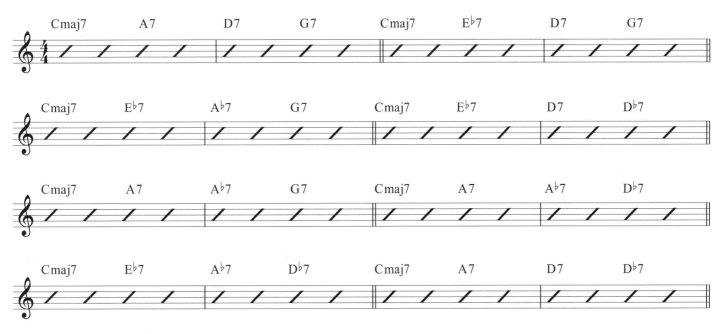

Tritone substitution can work even with changes of chord quality. The basic I–VI–II–V progression can mix minor seventh with dominant seventh chords. Four samples follow.

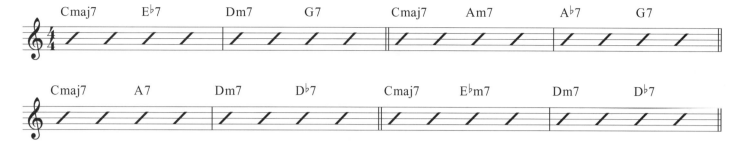

Notice that a chromatic progression can result from the substitution process. This brings us to the important harmonic concept of *fifth/half-step equivalence.* In any given progression involving dominant seventh chords, descending by fifth is functionally identical to descending by half step. This, of course, is possible through the principle of tritone substitution. The progressions below are all different but functionally interchangeable.

Bebop musicians often made use of harmonic embellishment, elaboration, and substitutions in their melodic lines. One could construct lines using these principles without having them played by the rhythm section accompaniment. One should keep in mind that jazz occurs rhythmically and harmonically on several different layers, and the harmonic implications of the melody do not always coincide with those of the harmonic accompaniment (see Chapter 5).

PRACTICE SUGGESTIONS

Take several tunes and reharmonize them using harmonic embellishment, elaboration, and substitution, as demonstrated above. One may use the lead sheets from the back of the book, or any pop standard or jazz tune. The player can preplan these changes or improvise them spontaneously.

CHAPTER 5
MELODY

The bebop language is replete with characteristic melodic figures consisting of patterns, motions, and colorations. Some of the more common are listed and described below.

Characteristic Figures and Patterns

Ascending Arpeggios

The ascending arpeggio is one of the most common bebop gestures. It can occur at any time and with any chord. It can begin on any chord tone, and it can consist of altered chord tones. These ascending arpeggios usually consist of four notes, but less or more notes are possible. This figure can be subdivided into four types:

BASIC ARPEGGIO

This is the basic arpeggio. It may consist of three, four, or more notes.

HALF-STEP PREFIX

Very often, the four-note ascending arpeggio idea is preceded by a stepwise prefix. This prefix is usually a half step below the first note of the arpeggio. Rhythmically, this figure often takes the form of an eighth note followed by an eighth-note triplet.

RHYTHMIC VARIATIONS

Other rhythms can be played for this figure. Below are a few variants of this common figure.

PREFIX VARIATIONS

The prefix can also be a whole step below the arpeggio or a half or whole step above the first note of the arpeggio. A few samples follow.

Ascending arpeggios (of any type) are usually followed by a descending motion that can consist of a scalar line, an arpeggio, or a combination of both.

Descending Scalar Lines

Descending scalar lines are often used. These lines can be chromatic, diatonic, or a combination of both.

CHROMATIC

These often consist of three to six notes in half-step relationships. They appear in almost any context and with any type of chord. They are often used to begin a phrase or as connecting material between other figures.

DIATONIC

Descending diatonic scalar lines are often played. They function in much the same contexts as chromatic lines.

COMBINATION

Chromatic and diatonic scales are often combined. They may follow one another or be mixed in various ways. Half steps can be inserted anywhere within a traditional diatonic scale, and it becomes difficult to analyze since one cannot always tell the difference between a passing tone and an extended chord tone. Such analyses are beyond the scope of this book. Suffice it to say that chromatic tones are freely used to ornament, decorate, embellish, and color scalar passages.

The following examples taken from bebop recordings make use of combined scalar lines.

Chromatic passing tone within a diatonic scale

TRACK 7

Chromatic followed by diatonic motion

TRACK 8

Chromatic followed by diatonic motion

TRACK 9

Combined Arpeggios & Scalar Lines

Scalar lines often follow ascending arpeggios. Below are several examples from bebop recordings with different types of scalar lines.

E♭ major scale

TRACK 10

B♮ passing tone inserted into B♭ major scale

TRACK 11

E♮ passing tone inserted into A♭ major scale

TRACK 12

Chromatic scale followed by diatonic motion

TRACK 13

Ascending Diminished Seventh

Another characteristic bebop harmonic-melodic device is the interval of an ascending diminished seventh. It is usually played as a simple two-note interval beginning on the third and ending on the flatted ninth of a dominant ♭9 chord. However, the interval may be filled in with arpeggiated notes.

The harmonic impulse of this interval in the context of a dominant seventh chord pushes toward to the chord of resolution. In the case of a G7♭9 as shown above, the third and flatted ninth of the G7 tend strongly toward the root and fifth of a chord that has C as its root. This common motion can occur on any primary or secondary dominant chord. A few examples from bebop recordings follow.

This excerpt begins with a major scale with a chromatic passing tone. The ascending diminished seventh occurs on a VI7 (F7), which goes to II7 (B♭7) in the key of A♭ major.

TRACK 14

The excerpt begins with a chromatic-diatonic scale line. As in the previous example, the ascending diminished seventh occurs on a VI7 (D7), which goes to II7 (G7) in the key of A♭ major.

TRACK 15

An ascending diminished seventh often occurs in the eighth measure of a blues when a VI7 (V of II) chord is present. The example here is played as a filled-in arpeggio.

TRACK 16

Here, the interval occurs on the V chord (F7) in the key of B♭ major.

TRACK 17

Notice, in the preceding examples, that the ascending diminished seventh leap is always followed by a descending line.

Descending Arpeggios

Bebop melodies use descending arpeggios, but not quite as often as ascending ones. One could make the generalization that ascending motions tend to be in thirds (arpeggios), and descending motions tend to be stepwise (scalar); of course, this is not always the case but merely a statistical observation. While descending arpeggiated figures are used often enough, they usually are not as distinctive as ascending arpeggios.

SEVENTH CHORDS

As with ascending arpeggios, descending arpeggios can be based on any part of an extended chord. Thus they can begin on any chord tone, chord extension, or alteration. Descending arpeggios are often used to imply substitute chords.

TRIADS

Triadic formations are often used as descending arpeggiated figures. These triadic formations are not necessarily formed from the basic chord triad but are more often derived from upper extensions. These formations give the same effect as superimposing a triad of a different chord on top of the prevailing harmony (polychords). In the following example, the implied triads are shown in parentheses.

The following examples taken from bebop recordings contain descending arpeggios combined with other figures.

A mostly chromatic scale is followed by a descending E♭ major triad arpeggio over an F7. This gives the effect of suspending the Cm7 into the next measure (see Chapter 3). The harmonic implications of the melodies are shown below the staff.

TRACK 18

An ascending arpeggiated line is soon followed by a descending A♭ major triad over a D7. Here the A♭ triad acts as a tritone sub for D7.

TRACK 19

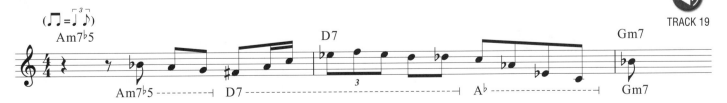

A descending diatonic scale is followed by a descending Gm7 arpeggio over a C7. The Gm7 arpeggio acts as a suspension of the Gm7 from the first measure.

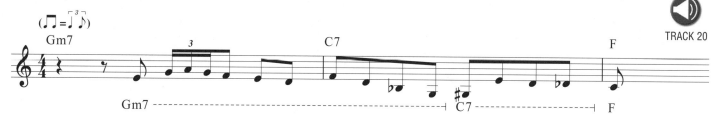

A descending Em triad arpeggio is followed by a descending Dm9 arpeggio in the following measure.

Descending arpeggios often follow ascending arpeggios, and sometimes a consistent up-and-down arpeggiated motion is produced. In this excerpt, the upper four notes of three successive ninth chords are arpeggiated for the first three chords and followed by a B♭ major triad arpeggio.

Complex sounds result from arpeggiated dissonant altered extensions. In this example, the substitutions are more implied than obviously stated. The D7 and G7 are both embellished melodically with an upper neighbor chord and a tritone sub. This example represents one of the hallmarks of the bebop style—melodic superimposition of harmonic embellishment, elaboration, and substitution on a level independent from the ongoing tune.

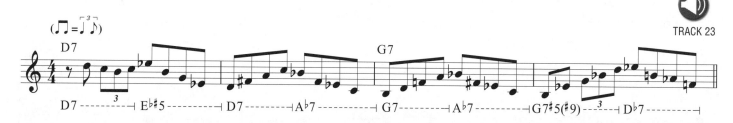

As the above example demonstrates, descending arpeggios are often used to emphatically indicate substitute chords. This next example clearly implies a C♯m7 chord substituting for a G7 (tritone). The C♯m7 begins on the fourth beat and overlaps into the first beat of the next measure.

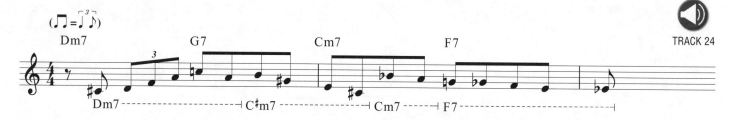

A descending C#maj7 arpeggio substitutes for the first two beats of the F7 (tritone). A descending Gm triad arpeggio on the F7 follows.

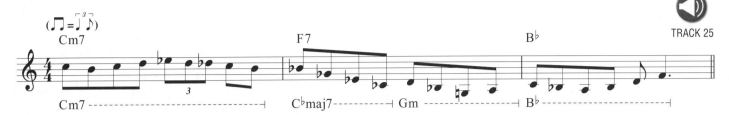

Ascending Scales

Ascending scales are sometimes used for bebop melodies but not nearly as often as descending scales. The scalar materials are usually diatonic with one or two chromatic passing tones. A few samples of ascending scalar lines combined with previously mentioned figures follow.

The following excerpt presents a straightforward ascending B♭ major scale with one chromatic passing tone.

The next example shows a simple ascending B♭ major scale followed by a descending B♭ major triad arpeggio on the F7. The B♭ triad functions as an anticipation of the B♭ chord. The descending Cm triad arpeggio and the F chord fragment played on the B♭ chord also functions as an anticipation of the next measure's chords. This is a great example of the bebop style's penchant for basing melodies on chords that are not necessarily present but anticipated or, in some cases, delayed.

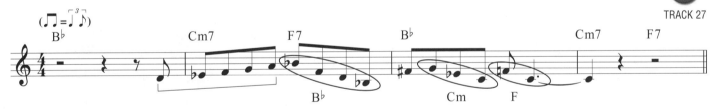

The next example begins with a descending Fm7♭5 arpeggio on a G7 chord, which makes for a G7♭9♭13 chord. A simple ascending diatonic scale fragment follows, which is then followed by a descending diatonic scale and a B♭m7 descending arpeggio on a C7 chord, which makes for a C7♭9♭13 chord.

The next example shows an F augmented triad in the first measure and an ascending chromatic scale in the third measure.

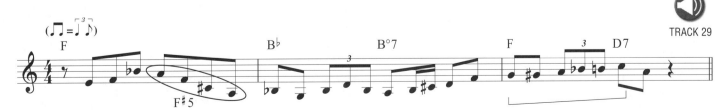

The next example begins with a descending scale fragment followed by an ascending arpeggio. This is followed by a descending Ab major triad arpeggio on a D7♭9 chord, which acts as a tritone sub leading to the Gm chord. Two ascending essentially diatonic scales follow.

TRACK 30

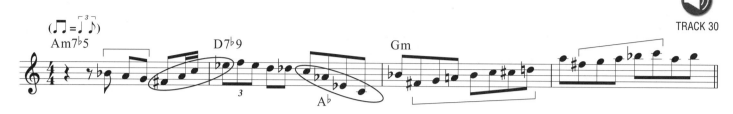

Ornaments

Bebop is a highly decorative music. Often, several notes are used to ornament a single pitch. These ornaments range from simple neighbor-note motions to complex decorations. While ornamentation colors the tonal/rhythmic palette of the music, the sum total of melodic motion is often zero. In other words, the music can be melodically static even though there are many notes played. Several ornamental processes are described below.

Neighboring Tones

Neighboring tones are auxiliary tones above or below a main note. Often, both are used, creating a "double neighbor." The following example shows various neighbor-note motions for the note C.

TRACK 31

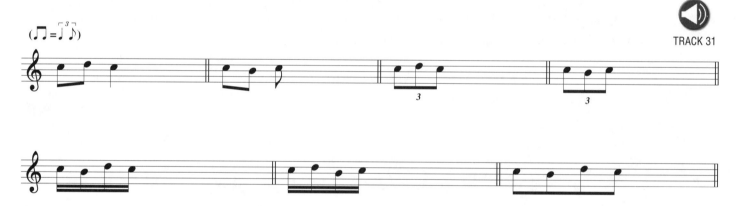

Turns

Turns are derived from neighboring notes—a main note is ornamented from both above and below, in either order, before returning to the main note. These ornaments "turn around" the main note. Turns are commonly used in bebop. A few samples follow.

TRACK 32

Turns and neighboring notes often occur before the main note first sounds. A few examples for the note C follow.

TRACK 33

Inverted Mordents

The most common single-note ornament used in bebop is the inverted mordent—a simple neighbor-note decoration, moving from the main note to the upper neighbor note and back. It usually occurs as a triplet figure, but other rhythms also are used. Most of the time, the figure leads to downward stepwise motion.

TRACK 34

Ornamentation of a single note can take many forms in bebop. Diatonic and chromatic embellishment are common. A few samples taken from recorded bebop performances follow.

TRACK 35

Ornamental Melody and Basic Pitch Motion

Music occurs on many levels. Melody can occur independently from harmony. For instance, when played alone, the melody exists as a relationship among the individual pitches projected rhythmically through time. These pitches also relate to a tonic or central pitch. When harmonies (chords) are added, however, each pitch also relates to the chord at hand. We now can also add the parameter of how each chord relates to each other and how each melody note not only relates to the chord that sounds with that note, but also how a melody note relates to the succeeding notes of different chords.

Melodies not only work on a note-to-note basis but also on a longer-term relationship of stepwise basic pitch motions. The basic pitch level ignores the foreground layer of activity (that which is actually heard) and functions on a more basic unadorned level of activity by reducing the melody to mostly stepwise connections. For instance, the following melody can be heard on two different levels. The melody is presented on its most foreground level above and on a background level below. Notice that, on a basic pitch level, the melody is simply moving down by step.

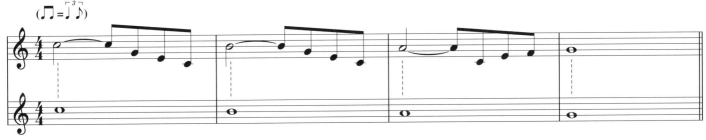

The basic pitch motion here is one that leads from one note to another by step. This can occur through ascending or descending motions by half steps and/or whole steps. The following examples are taken from recorded bebop performances. The basic pitch motion is indicated below each example. These are examples of ornamented stepwise motion.

Once the principle of single-note and stepwise ornamentation and decoration is understood, it is easy to extend this concept to include longer stepwise basic pitch lines. The next example shows connections of three or more basic pitches with ornamental melodies. The basic pitch outlines are shown below. Notice that basic pitch durations vary greatly. Note that in the last excerpt, the first note of the basic pitch line actually begins an octave lower, but the implied motion is still stepwise as indicated by the octaves. This is common and does not disrupt the sense of downward continuity.

TRACK 36

The following excerpts show some of the previously discussed bebop figures in combination with single-note and stepwise ornaments and decorations.

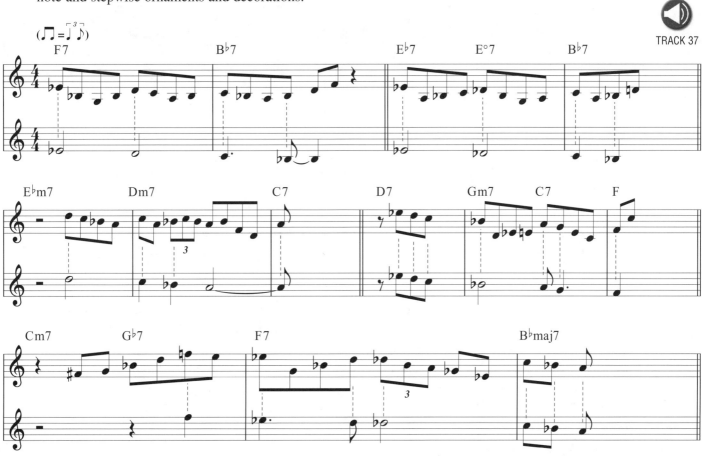

These next examples use ascending arpeggios and descending arpeggios.

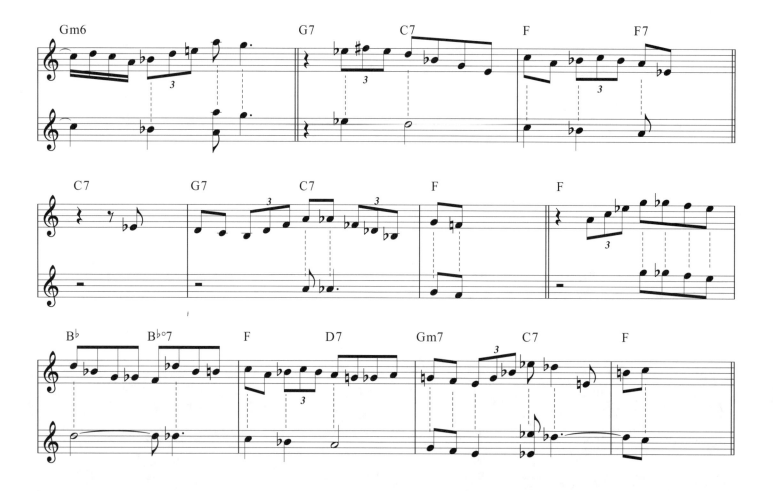

The concept of background stepwise pitch connections may seem to be overly analytical and complex, but close examination of the great bebop players' compositions and improvisations clearly reveals this process. A common question is, "Were they thinking about this as they were writing and playing?" The answer is most probably "no," but good music, regardless of era and style, almost always adheres to this principle. It can be found in Bach, Beethoven, Charlie Parker, Bud Powell, Miles Davis, etc. Great bebop, like any other great art form, is not a series of haphazard events. It is, rather, an intuitively created set of complex, but well-crafted relationships and ideas.

The next example shows how the concepts can be employed in a typical bebop melody.

PRACTICE SUGGESTIONS

Any or all of the figures, ornaments, or melodic excerpts can by practiced by playing them through the circle of fifths, whole step, and half-step cycles. See the practice suggestions in Chapter 3 for a description of these cycles. A few samples follow.

An ascending arpeggio figure with a half-step prefix is used as an example below. Since these figures are not specific to any particular chord, they can be practiced with several different chords. The figure below is presented with four different chords.

The reader should practice this figure with all four chords—and any other chords that seem compatible—through all of the cycles. An example through the descending circle of fifths follows.

This same cycle can be practiced with the other chords shown above. An example follows.

Any or all of the "combined figure" examples found in this chapter, or fragments of them, can be practiced through the cycles as well. An example found earlier of an ascending arpeggio soon followed by a descending triad arpeggio follows. The last note has been omitted from the original example to facilitate a smoother exercise. A descending whole-step cycle is used below. (In order to get all twelve keys, the same cycle is then repeated a half step higher.)

The reader should take any or all of the examples in the chapter and play them through all of the cycles.

Basic pitch motions and ornamentation can be practiced by setting up target notes (say, a descending chromatic scale) at regular time spans (say, the first beat of every measure) and playing connecting figures and ornaments in between them.

Chapter 6
SCALES AND TONALITY

Scale theories are somewhat new to jazz. The term *scale* is used in this context as a collection of notes (other than an arpeggio) that serves as source material for a melody or melodic idea. George Russell is probably most responsible for thinking of jazz improvisations as based on scales rather than chords; however, the concept did not take hold until the mid 1950s. Although the original bebop players are the first jazz players to base their improvised melodies more on scales than on chords, they did not consciously do so.

The approach taken in this book in one based on melodic/rhythmic ideas; nevertheless, thinking in terms of scales can be useful and instructive. Therefore, several scales will be discussed in relation to common bebop practice.

Diatonic material is common in bebop. Major scale material is often used on I chords. Most "inside" playing is done on I chords and tonic chord substitutes, or during basic diatonic progressions such as I-VI-II-V. Bebop melodies are somewhat tied to their underlying harmonic structure and often mirror the harmonic functions that coincide with them. Tonic chords (I chords) are the most stable and the most at rest. Dominant chords (V chords) are the most active and unstable. It is no coincidence that the most diatonic, "inside" melodies occur over tonic harmonies, and the most chromatic, "outside" melodies occur over dominant harmonies. Melodies that occur with subdominant harmonies (II or IV chords) tend to lie somewhere in between. The basic principle governing these generalizations is that of *tension and release.* Most music and most art forms of any kind rely on this principle. The artist creates tension and releases that tension in various ways. Some jazz has almost all tension with little release. Some types of "free jazz," for instance, are almost always tense. Other types of jazz can be played with almost no tension. "New age" jazz often falls into this category. Most other forms of jazz, however, make use of tension and release in various ways.

One should be mindful of the ways tension can be created and equally aware of the ways in which, once created, it can be released.

One common process is to start a solo in a rhythmically simple diatonic sort of way and gradually build up tension through ever-increasingly complex rhythms and harmonies. Other solos may go through relatively consistent ups and downs. The tunes themselves may have tension and release built into them, and players often play off these inherent polarities.

Diatonic Scales

Diatonic materials are those derived from the traditional seven-note scales—that is, the major scale and its derivative modes, plus the various forms of the minor scale.

The Major Scale (and Its Modes)

The derivative modes of the major scale are obtained by starting the scale from each successive note or degree, creating a set of derived scales—all using exact same pitches, but each emphasizing a different root (or tonic) and having a different quality, attributable to the different interval patterns. These derived scales are usually referred to as *modes* (coming from the traditional church modes). The major scale and its derivative modes are shown below, based in the key of C.

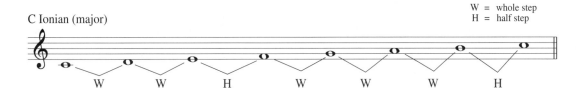

59

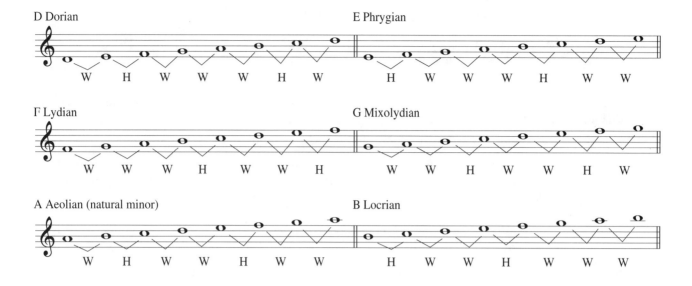

D Dorian   E Phrygian
W H W W W H W   H W W W H W W

F Lydian   G Mixolydian
W W W H W W H   W W H W W H W

A Aeolian (natural minor)   B Locrian
W H W W H W W   H W W H W W W

While some theorists think of the notes of a C major scale when played over a Dm7 chord as a D Dorian mode, implying D as a temporary tonic, the reality is that in this situation C is still the tonic, and thus a C major scale is still operating. No one would analyze a similar situation in music of Bach or Mozart in that manner, and there seems to be no need to do it in jazz other than to fit it into neat models for improvisation studies. The approach taken here for standard types of material is that of traditional practice. In other words, if a diatonic scale is played over a II–V–I progression in the key of C major, there would be one C major scale played over all three chords and not the three separate scales of C major, D Dorian, and G Mixolydian. Keys can change rapidly in bebop tunes, and it is simpler to think of each new key rather than each new chord as having a corresponding scale.

It should be noted that modes do come into play with later forms of jazz from the late 1950s (e.g., free jazz or modal jazz). Additionally, the great use of dominant seventh chords in blues tunes also allows for a modal (Mixolydian) approach and analysis.

The Minor Scales

Minor scales are also employed and come in three basic forms: natural (pure) minor, harmonic minor, and melodic minor. Since the melodic minor scale has differing ascending and descending forms, a fourth minor scale usually referred to as the "jazz minor" scale is sometimes added to the three traditional minor scales. The "jazz minor" scale is simply the ascending version of the melodic minor scale played both ascending and descending. All four minor scales for the tonic C are shown below.

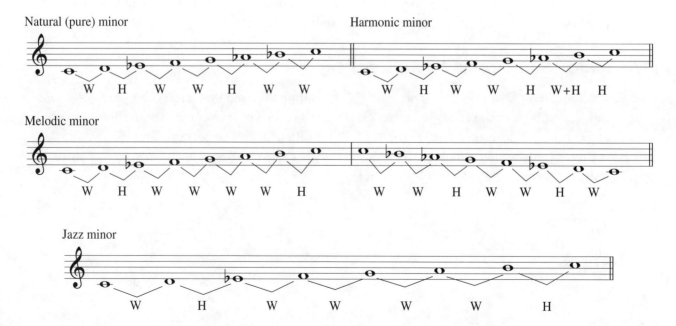

Natural (pure) minor   Harmonic minor
W H W W H W W   W H W W H W+H H

Melodic minor
W H W W W W H   W W H W W H W

Jazz minor
W H W W W W H

The real trick to improvising bebop—particularly when applying scales—is to know what key you are in at any given moment. In order to do this, one must be aware of how any given chord is functioning. The following chart lists some of the more common functions for naturally occurring diatonic chord types.

Chord Type	Function	Example
maj7 or 6	I or IV in major ♭III or ♭VI in minor	Cmaj7 = I in C major, IV in G major = ♭III in A minor, ♭VI in E minor
m7	II, III, or VI in major I or IV in minor	Cm7 = II in B♭ major, III in A♭ major, VI in E♭ major = I in C minor, IV in G minor
dom7	V in major or minor ♭VII in minor	C7 = V in F major or F minor = ♭VII in D minor
m(maj7)	I in minor	Cm(maj7) = I in C minor
m6	I or IV in minor	Cm6 = I in C minor, IV in G minor
m7♭5	II or VI in minor VII in major	Cm7♭5 = II in B♭ minor, VI in E♭ minor = VII in D♭ major
dim7	VII in major or minor, V chord sub, or passing chord	C°7 = VII in D♭ major or minor

Here is the same basic information but presented in another manner. Each chord type is shown according its position within a major or minor key. In bebop jazz, the I, II, and V chords are by far the most common harmonies and are the best indicator of key.

MAJOR

chord type:	maj7 or 6	m7	m7	maj7 or 6	dom7	m7	m7♭5 or dim7
function:	I	II	III	IV	V	VI	VII

MINOR

chord type:	m7, m(maj7) or m6	m7♭5	maj7 or 6	m7 or m6	dom7	maj7 or 6	m7♭5	dom7	dim7
function:	I	II	♭III	IV	V	♭VI	VI	♭VII	VII

The following example presents a relatively simple progression that changes keys several times. It is analyzed according to the principles given. The major or minor scales relative to each prevailing key can serve as diatonic source material for improvising over the progression.

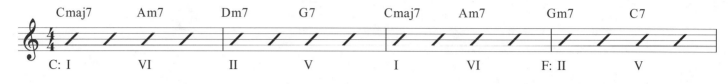

Often, sections of bebop melodies are made from simple diatonic scale material with occasional chromatic passing tones. A few excerpts from bebop recordings follow.

The following example is based completely on an E♭ major scale.

TRACK 40

The first part of the next example is also based on an E♭ major scale until the last beat of the first measure, where it anticipates the A♭7 chord and adjusts the G♮ to a G♭ and the D♮ to a D♭.

TRACK 41

Most bebop phrases make use of some type of chromatic inflection. The following example in E♭ major is essentially diatonic with two chromatic passing tones.

TRACK 42

The next passage goes through II-V progressions in three different keys (C, B♭, A♭) before ending on the notes D and F, anticipating a D7#9 chord.

TRACK 43

The Mixolydian Mode

The Mixolydian mode mentioned previously can serve as a tonality in itself, independent from a dominant functioning harmony.

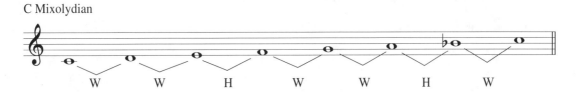

This is most often the case during a blues tune. I and IV chords, as well as V chords, are often dominant seventh chords. The blue-note coloration of the flat seventh lends itself to the use of this mode as opposed to the major scales.

The next passage is an F Mixolydian phrase from a blues tune.

TRACK 44

The Blues Scale

Blues scales are used most often during blues solos but can be interjected at any time. A typical bebop blues solo mixes blues licks with bebop melodies.

The traditional blues scale in C is as follows.

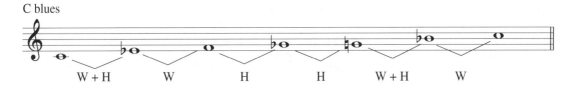

The blues scale originated in the mid-nineteenth century by African Americans, but its derivation is unknown. It is similar to a minor pentatonic scale but has one added half step in the middle. Traditional forms of blues such as country blues, city blues, etc. make great use of this scale. Rhythm 'n' blues, rock 'n' roll, as well as jazz, also rely on this scale. The curious aspect of the blues scale is that it is usually superimposed on harmonies derived from the major scale. Thus, there are several clashes between what are essentially two different tonalities. The following example shows the dichotomy.

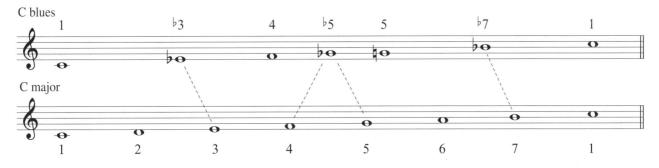

This duality of tonality clearly demonstrates the layering principle present in the blues. The harmonic layer proceeds on a different tonal plane from the melodic layer. The blues scale works no matter what the chord changes are. It is a horizontally conceived and perceived phenomenon. The vertical sonorities work on a different plane and relate more to themselves than to the melody. This essential principle, first found in early blues performances, is often carried over into other non-blues styles of jazz. Scales other than the blues scale can be applied in a similar way in various situations. This apparent ignoring of the changes was often employed by tenor saxophonist Lester Young during the 1930s and served as an inspiration to the early bebop players of the 1940s. A few examples of the use of the blues scale from bebop recordings follow.

The following excerpt makes use of a C blues scale.

TRACK 45

The next example is based on an F blues scale.

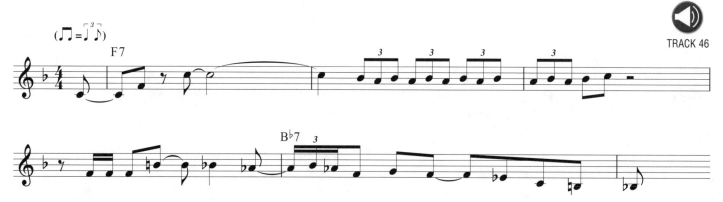

TRACK 46

The following excerpt uses the traditional blues scale exclusively until the fourth beat of the second measure.

TRACK 47

The Diminished Scale

The diminished scale is an artificial symmetrical scale comprising eight notes and consisting of alternating whole steps and half steps. It was first used in the early twentieth century by classical composers who referred to it as the octatonic scale. It is not clear if jazz musicians were consciously using it before the 1950s. The diminished scale has two forms: the whole-half version and the half-whole version. The whole-half diminished scale begins with a whole step and is typically used with a diminished chord. The half-whole diminished scale begins with a half step and is typically used with a dominant chord. These scales are shown below.

Dominant diminished scale (half-whole)

Diminished diminished scale (whole-half)

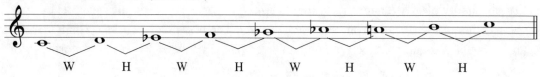

Both forms of the diminished scale are symmetrical, as are diminished seventh chords. And just as there are really only three different diminished chords (C–E♭–G♭–A, C♯–E–G–B♭, and D–F–A♭–B), there are only three different diminished scales. Each equivalent group contains the same notes but in different orders.

Using the dominant diminished scale provides an easy way of playing altered notes on a dominant chord. The dominant (half-whole) diminished scale provides notes for several altered and extended chord tones. A C dominant diminished scale can be rearranged to into the following chord. The added tones to the basic C7 are: ♭9, ♯9, ♯11, and 13.

Bebop musicians often made use of ♭9 and ♯9 in their playing. The dominant diminished scale provides both. A few examples showing use of the dominant diminished scale follow.

The following excerpt uses a G dominant diminished scale.

The next example uses a G dominant diminished scale for the first two measures. The diminished scale works well with the II–V in minor (Dm7♭5–G7♯9) even though the I chord is major (Cmaj7).

TRACK 49

The Altered Scale

The so-called *altered scale* is similar in some ways to the dominant diminished scale. Unlike the diminished scale, however, it is a seven-note scale that is derived from the melodic minor scale; it is one of the so-called modes of that scale.

Contemporary jazz theorists have derived modes from the melodic minor scale in the same way traditional theorists have derived the traditional modes from the major scale. The difference is that the modes from the melodic minor scale are not real tonalities as the traditional modes are. The melodic minor scale modes are scales that are superimposed onto existing tonalities. The Dorian mode, for example, can be superimposed onto a chord or tonality, but it also can be a tonality in itself; music can be in Dorian in the same way it can be in major or minor. The modes of the melodic minor scale do not function in this same way.

The altered scale (also know as super-Locrian) is derived from the seventh degree of the melodic minor scale. For example, one can obtain a C altered scale by beginning on the seventh degree of a C♯ melodic minor scale which is B♯, but enharmonically C♮. The following example shows this relationship. Note that the spellings for the altered scale are not strictly diatonic and may appear enharmonically as the context may dictate.

C# melodic minor scale   C altered scale (super Locrian)

W   H   W   W   W   W   H   H   W   H   W   W   W   W

Altered scales are generally used on dominant chords. The term "altered scale" comes from the fact that all tones that can be typically altered in a dominant chord are present in this scale. A C altered scale can be re-arranged into the following chord. The altered tones are: #5 or b13, b9, #9, #11.

C7b5(b9,#9,#11)

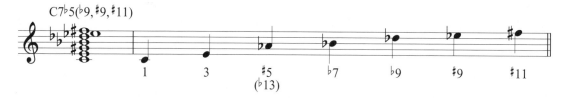

1   3   #5   b7   b9   #9   #11
         (b13)

The altered scale distinguishes itself from the dominant diminished by its inclusion of the #5 or b13, and its omission of the ♮13.

The following excerpt uses a C altered scale on the C7.

TRACK 50

The next excerpt uses a C altered scale on the C7.

TRACK 51

The Lydian Dominant Scale

The Lydian dominant scale, also known as Lydian b7, can also be derived from the ascending melodic minor scale—by starting from the fourth degree of that scale. For example, a C Lydian dominant scale can be produced by starting from the fourth degree of ascending G melodic minor. Some think of this scale as a Mixolydian mode with a raised fourth degree; others think of it as a Lydian mode with a lowered seventh degree.

G melodic minor scale   C Lydian dominant scale (Lydian b7)

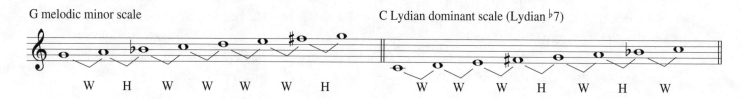

W   H   W   W   W   W   H   W   W   W   H   W   H   W

The Lydian dominant scale can be arranged into the following chord.

C13#11

1   3   5   b7   9   #11   13

56

This scale is most often used over dominant 7#11 chords and dominant 7♭5 chords. It gets frequent play on the secondary dominant chord, V7♭5 of V (II7♭5). In the following example, the scale is used over the D7♭5.

TRACK 52

The Whole Tone Scale

The whole tone scale is an artificial six-note symmetrical scale made up of all whole steps. Essentially, there are only two whole tone scales, since each uses half of all twelve available notes.

When used in isolation, a whole tone scale is really tonic-less, and thus there is no hierarchy of pitch relationships. French composer Claude Debussy was the first to make extensive use of this scale to create a sense of floating or ambiguous tonality. Jazz players typically superimpose a whole tone scale on a dominant 7♭5 or 7#5, in which case the tonal implications are assured by the dominant functioning chord. Thelonious Monk made the whole tone scale a personal cliché and often used it in isolation, independent of tonal function (see Chapter 10).

The following example uses a C whole tone scale on the C7#5.

TRACK 53

All tonal music is based on scales, and bebop is no exception. During their improvisations, bebop players thought more in scale terms than their predecessors, but the methodical application of certain scales to certain chord types is a more recent approach to improvisation; bebop players treated melody, harmony, and rhythm as parts of the same musical impulse, and rarely placed artificially derived constructs onto the musical discourse. In other words, the musical ideas and stylistic practice came first; the materials used were born of the process of improvisation and not chosen before the fact. One should keep this in mind when playing bebop as a living art form rather than an historical one.

PRACTICE SUGGESTIONS

All scales presented in this chapter should be practiced regularly. Four-octave separate hand practice is a good way to achieve fluency in these scales and is also a good way to develop technique in general.

Scales can also be practiced in cycles (see Chapter 3). Various patterns can be chosen and played through the cycles. Several scale patterns for a C major scale are shown below.

Play each of these patterns through all of the practice cycles. An example of the first pattern played through an ascending half-step cycle follows.

The reader should try to play all the scales used in this chapter as patterns through the practice cycles.

Chapter 7
COMPING

Comping refers to the playing of chords in a non-predictable manner while accompanying a melody. The term supposedly comes from the word "accompany" or "complement." The pianist can comp for other soloists using two-hand voicings or for a melodic line played by his or her own right hand using left-hand voicings. (See Chapter 3 for examples of bebop voicings.)

Most pianists before bebop did not comp but rather kept the pulse going in the left hand or in both hands. Steady quarter notes were the norm. A few Swing-era pianists began to comp chords, from time to time, to break up the sameness of steady quarter notes. Count Basie was the first pianist to consistently comp in the swing style. Earl Hines and Duke Ellington also contributed to this change of concept. Bebop pianists took their lead from Basie and others, and comping has become the norm ever since the early 1940s.

Comping usually consists of random-like chord punctuations that propel the music forward while supplying essential harmonic information. The trick to effective comping is knowing not only what to play but when to play it. The pianist should never lose sight of the fact that he or she is a member of the rhythm section. Even during solo piano playing, the bebop pianist thinks as if a rhythm section were present. The pianist, then, must choose appropriate voicings and appropriate times to play them.

Left-Handed

An example of left-hand comping follows. Notice how the left hand: 1) does not always play on the beat, 2) often plays when the right hand does not, and 3) rhythmically propels the music forward. Notice also the simple left-hand voicings. An important consideration is the durations of the chords. A mixture of longer and shorter durations adds variety to the accompaniment and rhythmic impulse of the music.

TRACK 54

The next example has a different, less busy kind of melodic line. Notice how the left hand adapts accordingly. The left hand often anticipates the chords by a half of a beat.

TRACK 55

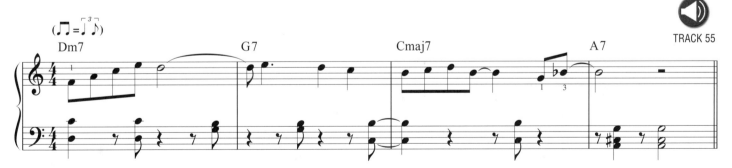

While comping, chords often come slightly before or after the beat that they are associated with. One should consider the *composite rhythm* and the overall flow of the melody when choosing where to place chords. The composite rhythm is the rhythmic totality of all of the simultaneous parts. If the left hand always plays when the right hand does, the composite rhythm is not changed. However, whenever the left hand plays when the right hand does not, the composite rhythm is increased.

There are times when one might consider a consistent, repetitive comping rhythm. An example of a typical consistent comping rhythm follows.

TRACK 56

Anther common rhythmic device is the consistent anticipation of beats 1 and 3. This was a favored device used by Red Garland and Ahmad Jamal.

TRACK 57

Although consistent comp rhythms can be used from time to time, random-like punctuations are more typical of an authentic bebop style.

Two-Handed

Two-handed comping presents some different challenges. The pianist now must accompany someone else's melodic lines. The same rhythmic and harmonic considerations must still be addressed, but now the pianist does not know exactly what lines will be played. Experience plays a big part in developing one's skill as an accompanist, as one must anticipate what the other musicians might play. Style has much to do with what one might expect to hear from certain players and performances. The pianist must anticipate not only what the soloist will play rhythmically but also harmonically. This involves chord extensions and alterations as well as substitute chords. One should try to hear where the soloist is going and know when to play a $\flat9$ or a $\sharp5$, etc.

Below are examples of how one might comp with two hands for the same lines given in the previous left-hand comping examples.

TRACK 58

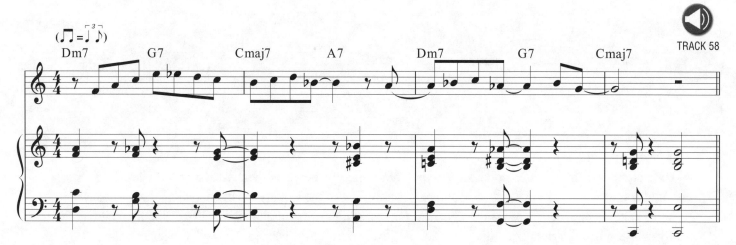

The following example shows a sample comping part on a typical bebop chord progression known as "rhythm changes" (see Chapter 8). Notice the rhythmic variations on the repeats of the same chord changes, and the harmonic embellishments, elaborations, and substitutions. Notice also the variety of voicings used.

TRACK 62

Texture, tessitura, rhythm, and voicings are important to consider when comping for another player. The jazz pianist should take comping seriously. It is one of the most important duties that he or she performs, whether for instrumentalists or singers. Jazz pianists should never lose sight of the fact that they are part of the rhythm section, as well as soloists.

Chapter 8 will offer many examples of left-hand comping for tunes in the bebop style. The reader should apply these principles to two-hand comping, as well.

PRACTICE SUGGESTIONS

Comping can be practiced by playing through the chord changes to a variety of tunes. Also, one can comp common chord progressions, such as II–V–I, through all of the practice cycles (see practice suggestions from Chapter 3). See "Lead Sheets" at the back of the book for instructions on how to use the play-along portion of the accompanying CD for practicing comping.

Chapter 8
CHARACTERISTIC TUNES

The bebop repertoire consisted of three basic kinds of material: blues tunes, pop standards, and original tunes. The original tunes were newly composed melodies based on pop standard forms and chord progressions.

A few samples of bebop-style tunes written for two hands follow. Lead sheets for all of these tunes are included at the end of the book.

Blues

Chord Progressions

Reharmonization of the basic twelve-bar blues progression was prevalent during the bebop era. The simple twelve-bar structure of blues serves as a model for almost infinite variation. The following example presents a very basic blues progression followed by ever-increasing reharmonizations. Notice the use of II-V progressions and tritone substitutions (see Chapter 4).

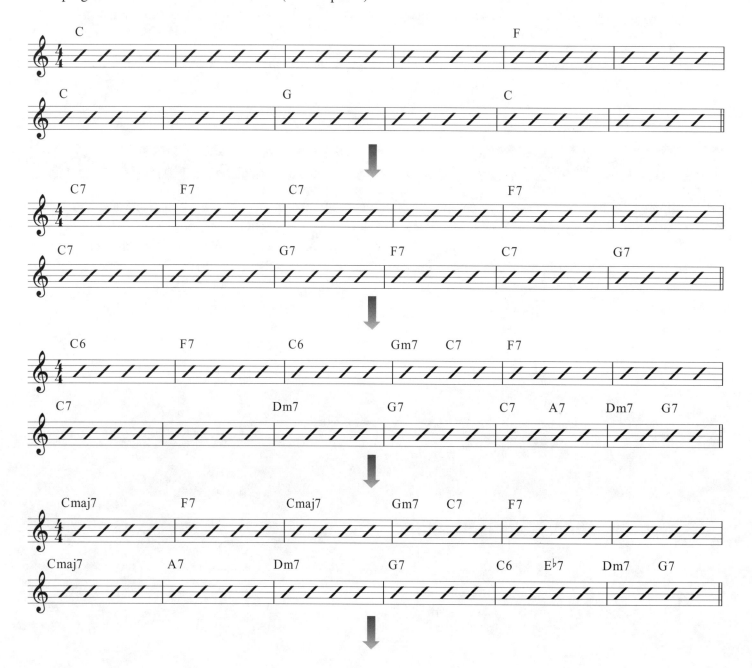

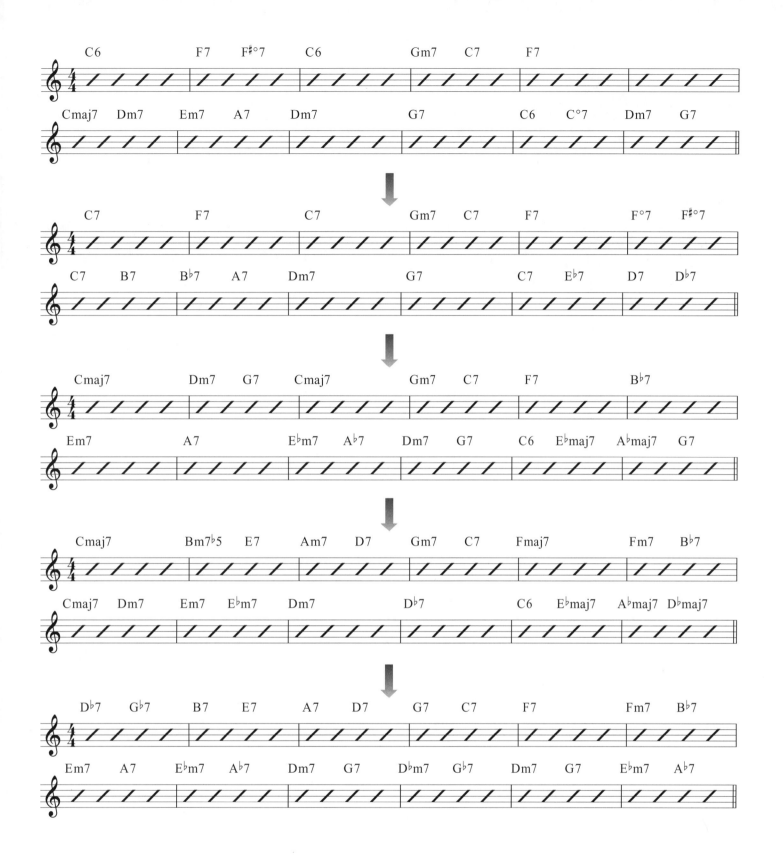

There are many more possible variations on the twelve-bar blues. These alternate progressions could be preplanned or spontaneously played. During any given performance, any number of different progressions could be used. Any member of the group may initiate substitute changes. The pianist should listen carefully and try to hear where the soloist may be going. The pianist may, at times, even nudge the soloist into certain harmonic areas and progressions.

Melodies

Traditional blues melodies make much use of the blues scale (see Chapter 6). Bebop blues melodies are usually very different from other blues melodies. Traditional blues melodies are based on the text (lyrics) form of AAB. There are three phrases, and each lasts for four measures. The second phrase repeats the first and is followed by a different third phrase. This form is generally used in country blues, folk blues, rhythm 'n' blues, rock blues, and various types of jazz blues. An example of this basic melodic form with a standard set of blues changes follows.

Basic Blues

TRACK 63

Blues tunes were used often in the Swing era but were smoothed out somewhat. The chords were more fluid, and the instrumental melodies tended to be in the form of AAA. Here, there was only one phrase that was played three times. This fit in nicely with the swing style's emphasis on riffs. *Riffs* are repeated short melodic patterns with catchy rhythms. A riff blues could have six statements of the riff, which breaks each phrase into two statements. Slight changes were made to accommodate the changing chords. The following is an example of a swing blues.

Swing Blues

TRACK 64

Bebop musicians retained the basic twelve-bar formal structure of the blues and a semblance of the blues scale from time to time but infused the music with typical bebop melodies and rhythms. Bebop blues tunes tend to be *through-composed* with no real repeats. Like other original bebop tunes, they sound similar to improvisations. The harmonic progressions can be basic or more complex. A blues in bebop style with left-hand comping follows. (See the end of this book for the lead sheet.)

CLUE'S BLUES

Bebop Blues

Pop Standards & Original Tunes

Pop standards written during the 1920s, '30s, and '40s served as source material for bebop performances in many ways: 1) the songs themselves were often played and served as points of departure for improvisations; 2) the melodies to these standards were often discarded, while the chord progressions served as harmonic structures for new original melodies; and 3) even totally original non-blues bebop tunes were based on the formal structures and same types of progressions as the pop standards.

Pop standards were the dominant type of popular music during the 1920s, '30s, and '40s. Some of these songs were jazz-based, and some were not. Jazz musicians from this time, however, turned almost any song into a jazz tune by "jazzing it up." Many of the hits of the Swing era were still played by bebop players, but typically they added more complex chords and chord progressions.

A typical pop standard has a 32-measure form. Most of these forms fall into one of three patterns, in order of most common usage:

- **AABA:** The first eight-measure section (A) is played once through, then repeated. A contrasting section (B) follows, after which the first section (A) is repeated again. Some of the A sections may have slight variations in them.

- **ABAB′:** The first section (A) is followed immediately by a contrasting section (B). Then the first section returns, followed by an obvious variation on the B section. (The mark " ′ " or the number "1" is used to denote a variation; one calls this "B prime." Successive numbers can be used to denote different variations.)

- **ABAC:** This form has only one repeating section and, not coincidentally, is the least used of the three.

Other forms are possible, such as ABCD, but these are relatively rare.

When bebop musicians played a pop standard, they most often modified or added chord changes to the original harmonic progressions (see Chapter 4). When bebop composers based a new tune on a pop standard, they often did the same. Certain pop standards were favored over others for the adoption of new melodies. George and Ira Gershwin's "I Got Rhythm" was by far the most often used model. So many bebop tunes are based on this pop standard that musicians refer to the harmonic progression simply as "rhythm changes," which is short for "I Got Rhythm" changes. Thus if one knows "rhythm changes," one knows the chord progression to hundreds of jazz tunes.

Like everything else in jazz, nothing is sacred, and there are countless variations on the basic "rhythm changes" progression. "Rhythm changes" are usually but not exclusively played in B♭. The form is AABA. The A sections hover around I (B♭) and move to IV (E♭) before coming back to I (B♭). The B section (bridge) moves down a circle of fifths starting on III7 (D7).

Three variations on "rhythm changes" follow. They are presented below each other for comparison. Notice the typical harmonic substitutions and embellishments used.

Rhythm Changes

The following tune is based on "rhythm changes." (See the end of the book for the lead sheet.)

ENDOCRINOLOGY

The next tune is based on the changes to Duke Ellington's "Perdido." This swing classic served as a model for many bebop tunes. The form is AABA. The A sections are based on a simple II-V-I turnaround formula progression. The B section is the same as the B section for "rhythm changes" and is based on a series of dominant chords going down the circle of fifths from III7.

PER DIEM

TRACK 67

The next tune is based on Cole Porter's "What Is This Thing Called Love." The unusual mixture of minor and major progressions offers an ambiguous tonality that appealed to bebop players. "What Is This?" is almost a through-composed tune, in that there are no exact sectional repeats. Although the harmonic form is AABA, the melody might be considered ABCA'. The last A section is actually a combination of sections A and B. Notice the phrasing across the harmonic cadences.

WHAT IS THIS?

TRACK 68

The next tune is based on Tadd Dammeron's "Lady Bird," an original bebop tune. The form is only sixteen measures long and is completely through-composed. The last two measures feature Dammeron's famous I–♭III–♭VI–♭II turnaround consisting of all major seventh chords.

The derivative tune presented here offers an example of harmonic embellishment. Notice the appoggiatura chords in measures 3 and 7, and the anticipated appoggiatura embellishment in measure 12.

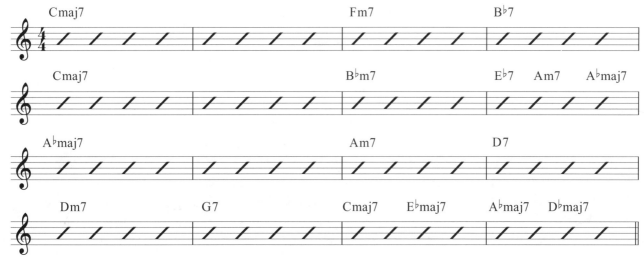

LADYBUG

TRACK 69

PRACTICE SUGGESTIONS

Play the tunes in this chapter as written. After learning each tune, refer to the end of the book and play it from the lead sheet, improvising left-hand comping. Then, improvise on the chords and form of the tune. Finally, use the play-along portion of the CD to listen to and play along with a bebop combo.

Chapter 9
BUD POWELL

Bud Powell (1924-1966) was *the* most imitated and influential bebop pianist. He had an astounding technique that could match swing great Art Tatum's virtuosity. Although he was not one of the inventors of bebop, he learned the style early on and became its leading representative. Thelonious Monk, one of the founding fathers of bebop, took the young Powell under his wing and tutored him in the new jazz language. While Monk wandered off into his own unique idiosyncratic style, it was Powell, coming under the spell of Charlie Parker, who most successfully adapted the bebop horn player's approach to the piano. Like most music innovators, Powell mastered and could play in the older style swing. In fact, much of his ballad playing is in a pure swing style reminiscent of Art Tatum.

Most of the preceding material in this book relates directly to Bud Powell's playing. The typical bebop piano style is directly rooted in his approach. Everything from chord voicings and comping rhythms to phrasing, melodic rhythms, and accents, is found in and influenced by Powell's playing. He was to pianists what Charlie Parker was to saxophonists. Like Parker, Powell often played a series of short "incomplete" phrases before unleashing a long steady stream of mostly eighth notes. Some of Powell's lines are extremely long but usually coherent and unified on a background level by stepwise basic pitch motions (see Chapter 5). He often played extremely fast double-time lines in sixteenth notes.

Bud Powell was a prolific composer and wrote some bebop classics and standards. His tunes often contain unusual harmonic and melodic twists. Two tunes in Bud Powell style follow. Each contains a head and a sample improvised chorus in his style.

The first tune is in AABA form. It has a four-measure introduction and sample improvisation for one chorus. It features the kind of shifting II-V progressions that Powell liked to use in his tunes.

BUDDING

TRACK 70

The next tune features some chromatic chord movement as well as shifting II-V progressions. The form is AABA, and the tune is slightly blues-like.

APPARITIONS

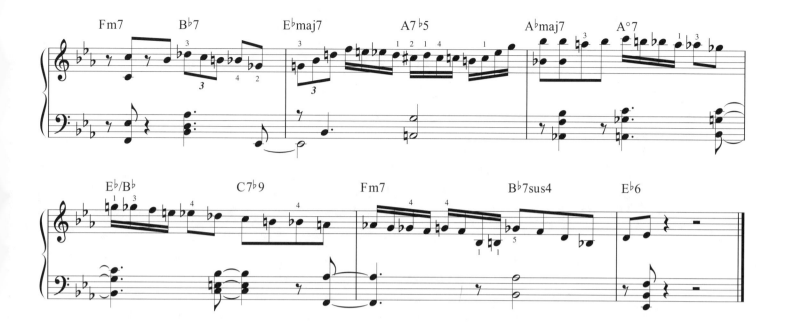

PRACTICE SUGGESTIONS

Play the tunes in this chapter as written. After learning each tune, refer to the end of the book and play from it the lead sheet, improvising left-hand comping. Then, improvise on the chords and form of the tune. Try to simulate Bud Powell's left-hand comping and right-hand approach to improvisation.

Chapter 10
THELONIOUS MONK

Thelonious Monk remains an enigma in the history of jazz. Although he was one of the inventors of bebop, he never became a real bebop player. His ideas on chord voicings and harmony left a lasting influence on bebop, but his piano style was unique and lay outside any style category of jazz. However, he performed mostly with bebop musicians and composed a wealth of tunes that were performed by bebop players. Unlike his protégé Bud Powell, Monk's playing does not fit neatly into the stylistic traits described in this book. Therefore, a few of Monk's more characteristic traits will be described here with examples.

The bebop piano concept of stripping chords down to two notes played by the left hand stems from Monk's early playing. He also evolved other unique ways of voicing chords that featured some stark dissonances. Rather than incorporate extended and altered tones into the context of a full chord, Monk would often expose them without the softening effect of the other chord tones. On the other hand, he also played dense, dissonant clusters. A few examples follow.

Monk's playing was unusually spare. Silence was a key ingredient. Various ideas could be separated by stretches of silence. Often, he played melodic lines with no chordal accompaniment. When he comped for

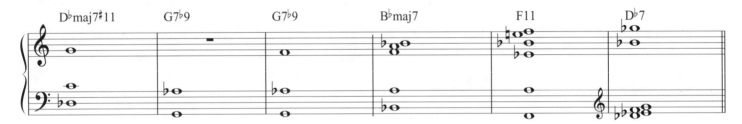

other soloists, he either played well-timed percussive punctuations or counter-melodies, often derived thematically from the tune. Often he would play nothing at all during all or part of another's solo.

Monk's melodies were usually angular with odd twists and turns. His improvised and written melodies were often based on one or two ideas. He would use these ideas as motives that served as seeds to spawn continuous variations on and/or for the development of ideas. A simple interval might serve as a motive in some cases. The use of space to separate thematic statements makes this process quite audible.

Perhaps the most peculiar aspect of Monk's playing was his rhythmic conception. His playing did not "swing" in any conventional way—swing style or bebop. His phrasing is difficult to describe. It sometimes seems to be operating in another time dimension from the rest of the band. He sometimes lagged far behind the beat. He was fond of *rhythmic displacement,* which is the playing of similar ideas on different parts of the measure. An example of this device follows.

TRACK 72

Monk used several musical devices that became associated with his style. He had a penchant for inserting whole-tone runs almost anywhere during a solo and often at endings. He also often played trills during solos. He frequently gave the illusion of bending notes by crushing minor seconds together and releasing one of the notes, or by holding a note while playing a minor second above or below. He played some of his melodies in parallel sixths. Examples of these devices follow.

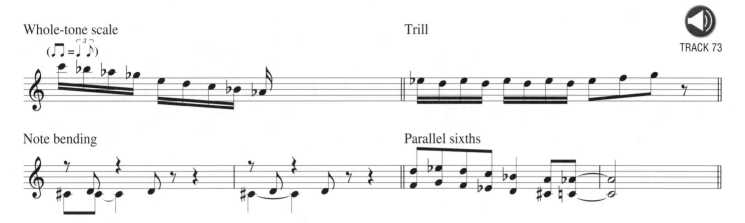

TRACK 73

Monk was a great composer in the real sense of the word. His tunes were true compositions and not just simply melodies. Most jazz tunes serve as heads or interesting points of departure for improvisation. Within the confines of a twelve-bar blues or a thirty-two bar pop song form, Monk wrote miniature compositional masterpieces that compare with any of the great classical works in terms of unity, relationships, and imagination. Indeed, his works are admired in the classical world for these very reasons. Most of his works are based on one or two ideas. He ingeniously expounds on one idea or exploits the relationship between two ideas by juxtaposing or integrating them. Monk wrote some tunes based on pop standard progressions as well as on original progressions.

Monk tunes are usually difficult to improvise on because of the their unusual harmonic motions and their quirky yet distinctive melodies. It is often said that, unlike most jazz tunes, one must know the melody of a Monk tune in order to improvise on it. The chord changes and the melodies are so inexorably tied that they cannot be separated.

Two tunes with sample improvisations in Monk's style follow.

Monk wrote many blues tunes. The following tune is a twelve-bar blues in Monk's style. It is followed by a two-chorus sample improvisation.

MONK-A-NING

TRACK 74

The next example is in a 32-measure AABA pop song form.

MONK'S CORNER

PRACTICE SUGGESTIONS

Play the tunes in this chapter as written. After learning each tune, refer to the end of the book and play from it the lead sheet, improvising left-hand comping. Then, improvise on the chords and form of the tune. Try to simulate Thelonius Monk's left-hand comping and right-hand approach to improvisation.

LEAD SHEETS

All of the tunes from Chapters 8, 9, and 10 are presented here in lead sheet form. The reader should play through the fully written-out versions in the previous chapters and then play in a similar style from these lead sheets. The lead sheets offer a way for the reader to practice creating accompaniments (comping) and improvising on the tunes. The tunes can be used to practice chord voicings, as well.

What's a Lead Sheet?

The *lead sheet* is the typical "score" used in small group jazz. It gives the melody and chord changes of a tune but offers no specific way to play it. All players read from the same lead sheet, and it is up to each individual musician to play material appropriate for his or her role in the band. The bassist improvises a bass line, the pianist comps on the chord changes, the horns play the melody as written or variations on the melody, and some or all players improvise new melodies to go along with the chords and form of the tune. Thus, from just a sketch, jazz musicians can fashion an entire performance.

Although bebop is a melodically, harmonically, and rhythmically complicated music, its formal procedure is quite simple. Practically all pure bebop arrangements are the same. The simple formula is "head–solos–head." The term *head* refers to the tune itself, the written or preplanned music (i.e., what appears on the lead sheet). The typical bebop performance consists of playing of the head in unison by one or several lead instruments (saxophone and trumpet, for example—or piano, if it's the main instrument). This is followed by several choruses of solo improvisation based on the chords and form of the head. There may or may not be a set limit to the number of choruses each soloist takes. After all of the solos are completed, the head is played again in unison as it was at the beginning. Sometimes, introductions and endings are added to the performance.

Playing Along with the CD Tracks

The first five lead sheets—the "characteristic tunes" from Chapter 8—are recorded on the accompanying CD. The band is a classic bebop quartet consisting of saxophone, piano, bass, and drums. The piano is isolated on the right stereo channel, and the rest of the band is on the left stereo channel. The reader should listen to each track in full stereo and then turn down the right channel (piano) in order to play along with the track. Assume the role of the pianist by comping during the heads and solos and improvising during the piano solo choruses. By listening to and then playing with a bebop band, the reader should acquire a sense of the bebop style and a sense of playing with a live band. (By listening to the right channel alone, the reader can focus on the piano's comping and improvisations.)

"CLUE'S BLUES" AND "LADY BUG"

Since the heads for these tunes are relatively short—12 bars and 16 bars, respectively—they are played twice at the beginning and end.

Head (sax)	2 choruses
Sax solo	3 choruses
Piano solo	3 choruses
Head	2 choruses

"ENDOCRINOLOGY," "PER DIEM," AND "WHAT IS THIS?"

The heads for these tunes are played only once at the beginning and end.

Head (sax)	1 chorus
Sax solo	2 choruses
Piano solo	2 choruses
Head	1 choruses

CLUE'S BLUES

JOHN VALERIO

LADY BUG

TRACK 77

JOHN VALERIO

ENDOCRINOLOGY

TRACK 78

JOHN VALERIO

Per Diem

John Valerio

WHAT IS THIS

John Valerio

Budding

Apparitions

John Valerio

Monk-a-Ning

John Valerio

Monk's Corner

John Valerio